Passing on the gift

The Story of Dan West

Passing on the gift

The Story of Dan West

by GLEE YODER

 THE BRETHREN PRESS, ELGIN, ILL.

The poem by Dan West entitled "Cross" appeared originally in the
June 18, 1947 issue of *The Christian Century*. It is copyright 1947 by
the Christian Century Foundation and is used by permission. The
poem appears on page 16.

Library of Congress Cataloging in Publication Data

Yoder, Glee.
    Passing on the gift.

    1. West, Daniel, 1893-1971. 2. Church of the
Brethren—Biography. I. Title.
BX7843.W46Y62   286'.5 [B]   78-6291
ISBN 0-87178-689-3

Preface

Each of us inherits a legacy from our families, our communities, our churches, our nation, our world. This legacy is ours to remember, to celebrate, to understand, to interpret, and to continue. Each of us is both critical and appreciative of the past that has been willed to us.

History is an objective "telling it like it was." Heritage is that part of our appropriation from the past which guides us in making decisions reflecting our faith and applying them in practical situations. *Passing on the Gift* is both a history and a heritage. It provides a partial history of an era and its influence, and of a man who lived in that particular time and place. But it also celebrates a heritage to be received, enjoyed, and passed on.

As his biographer I have been impressed anew by Dan West's commitment and advocacies. I join with the dozens who wrote about him and the thousands who feel, "My life will never be the same since Dan's touched mine."

My special thanks and appreciation to the following: to Lucille Rupel, Dan's widow, and their five children, Joel, Jan, Phil, Larry, and Steve, for their support, trust, and openness; to Gordon, my understanding husband, for his encouragement and reassurance; and to the many, many people who shared, through letters and interviews, their experiences and feelings about Dan.

The various resources in the library and files at the General Offices of the Church of the Brethren in Elgin, Illinois, provided much of the historical facts and background. I found especially helpful the historical survey by Roger Sappington entitled *Brethren Social Policy,* 1908-1958 (Brethren Press, 1961), and several magazine articles as well as the book *The God in You,* (University of Chicago Press, 1954) written by Dan's friend, Kermit Eby.

Because of the overlapping of the various movements in which Dan was involved, the story is arranged both chronologically and topically. The calendar of events will aid in keeping them in a proper perspective.

Glee Yoder

Booklets and Pamphlets by Dan West

The Coming Brotherhood, 1938, published by the Board of Christian Education, Church of the Brethren

Brethren Community Service, 1943, Board of Christian Education, Church of the Brethren

Thinking Together, 1948, Christian Education Commission, General Brotherhood Board, Church of the Brethren

Peace Education in Homes, 1956, Brethren Service Commission, General Brotherhood Board, Church of the Brethren

Peace Education in Churches (Dan West and Others), 1957, Brethren Service Commission, General Brotherhood Board, Church of the Brethren

Contents

Left, Dan and Lucille West; below, the five West children on Daisy; at bottom, the West farm at Middlebury, Ind.

A Calendar of Events

Dec. 31, 1893:	Birth of Dan West in Preble County, Ohio
1911:	Graduation from Pleasant Hill High School
1912-1913:	Attendance at Bethany Bible School
1917:	Graduation from Manchester College
1917-1918:	Service in the U.S. Army as a conscientious objector
1918-1930:	Teaching in various high schools; leadership in camps during the summers
1930-1936:	National director of young people's work, Church of the Brethren
Oct. 8, 1932:	Wedding of Daniel West and Lucille Sherck
July 21, 1934:	Birth of first child, Joel.
1936:	Worked for the Emergency Peace Campaign
Aug. 30, 1936:	Birth of daughter, Janet.
1937—1938:	Service in Spain as relief worker during Spanish Civil War
Oct. 4, 1938:	Birth of twins, Philip and Lawrence.
June 1942:	Heifers for Relief approved as a national project.
May 22, 1943:	Birth of Steven.
Jan. 1944:	Heifer Project Committee and UNRRA agree to cooperate in shipment of heifers
June 14, 1944:	First shipment of heifers, to Puerto Rico
June 1948:	Brethren Volunteer Service initiated
1959:	Retirement from Church of the Brethren staff
1959—1960:	Trip around the world
June 1960:	First lay moderator, Annual Conference, Church of the Brethren, Louisville, Kentucky
Winter 1968:	Disease diagnosed as Amytrophic Lateral Schlerosis
July 12, 1969:	25th anniversary of Heifer Project
Feb. 2, 1970:	Gastrostomy performed on Dan
Jan. 7, 1971:	Death of Dan West
July 2, 1977:	Dedication of "Dan West Acres" at Heifer Project International Ranch

Above, Dan as summer camp leader in the 1920's; right, first lay moderator of Annual Conference; below, dedication of a heifer and her offspring in Europe.

1
The Man Who Asked
and Asked

Tall, thin, with his shirt open at the neck, he told the story of a small boy who looked at a cupful of milk and asked, "How deep may I drink?" Searchingly he asked, "Do we have the right to eat cake when people do not have bread and milk?"

With chalk in hand he drew circles within circles. "In your circle of friendship where would you put the Negro, the Indian, the migrant worker?"

From the ground he picked up a splintered stick, symbol of the broken relationship between persons. "What are the steps toward forgiveness and reconciliation?"

Under an almond tree in Spain, haunted by the look on faces of hungry children, he pondered, "Wouldn't it be better to send them cows that would provide an ongoing supply of milk rather than continuing to send powdered milk?"

Writing on a dinner napkin in the hospital when he could no longer speak, he was still asking of himself and others the perennial question, "What do you think the church should be like five, ten years from now?"

Questions! Questions! Why? Why? He asked himself

questions over and over again. He put questions to everyone he met.

This prober, stimulator, inspirer, innovator, this prodder, this curious, creative, challenging person was Dan West. If he's a stranger to you, you must get to know him. Though he is no longer living, he may baffle you, but he will intrigue you. He may irritate you, but he will dare you. He may challenge your pattern of life, but you cannot forget what he says. Regardless of your various reactions to Dan West, you will come to love and to respect him.

An avid recyclist long before it became popular, Dan insisted that his family save all the so-called junk that other people threw away because "it might come in handy sometime." Almost everything on the farm which they owned was saved and recycled until it was completely used up. Tools were kept sharp, broken handles replaced, every item was cleaned and stored properly to assure long use. Clothes were practical, handed down, and worn out.

At the age of five, Joel, Dan's son, was assigned the task of sorting nails, his contribution to a building project that involved tearing down walls and rearranging partitions. A lot of nails were scattered around. It was Joel's job to decide whether they could be used without rebending, whether they could be rebent, or whether they were just too far gone and could be eliminated. Such frugality was often a nuisance to the West children but later the wise use of money and materials became part of their philosophy.

Dan's ecological concerns sometimes got in the way of efficient farming. A small plot of an acre and a half, very close to one of the barns, had a rather steep slope. Instead of simply planting Sudan grass for summer foliage for the animals, or hay such as alfalfa or timothy, Dan had read about a new crop, Bird's Foot Trefoil. It was a legume and was supposed to be better than clover and better for the soil. He spent a lot of time and energy just locating the seed. In a sense his ecological concerns included doing things experimentally, even when that might have interfered with the economic or the time factor in terms of profitable farming.

Feeling empathy and sympathy for the suffering people

of the world, Dan served as a relief worker in Spain during its horrible Civil War. There his dream of sending heifers to supply milk to starving children was born. Heifers for Relief International is the organization that has grown from one man's dream; a small committee project became a movement with worldwide recognition. The man had a dream—an impossible dream, many thought—but it became a reality.

Believing that changed people could change the world, Dan traveled up and down the country often challenging, "You twenty in this room could change the world!" Saying this over and over again, he combined it with the refrain of the Negro spiritual, "I Know the Lord Has Laid His Hands on Me." The repetition of such challenges, the silences, the daring of his ideas combined to make a meaningful commitment experience for those who heard him.

Dan was a Pied Piper who attracted idealistic youth. His strong faith, his love for God, for the church, and for persons offered them the solid foundation of belief they were seeking in a world of constant change. He encouraged youth to stand on their own two feet and to argue for their convictions. He trusted them at a time when many adults thought youth had misplaced values. While challenging to other youth, he sometimes produced the uneasy feeling in his own children that they did not live up to his expectations, for he often said, "A son should be taller than his dad."

Dan was a prophet. Prophets are "why" people, not "how" people. Popular as they travel espousing their causes, they are often hard to live with at home and at work. Ideas and ideals abound, but organizational insights and skills may be lacking; their expectations of themselves and of others are very high. While Dan often had his head in the clouds, he was realistic enough to keep his feet—though at times they were feet of clay—on the ground. He found the role of prophet sometimes uncomfortable and perplexing. But the members of his family understood and could talk about it, laugh about it, even differ with his thinking. Though his co-workers found him difficult at times, his ever probing, ever prodding question, "Why not?" kept the vision of the impossible before them as a possibility. In reflective moments his colleagues would acknowledge that Dan was Dan, and they would accept him with all virtues and limitations.

Dan's statements were provocative. "I cannot eat cake when others in the world do not have bread," was his trademark. "When I see so much that the war makers are doing and so little that the peacemakers are doing, I wonder why the difference. Find me one hundred young persons between the ages of twenty-one and thirty who will give as much for peace as a soldier gives for war, and we will change the thinking of Congress in three years' time."

Like an itinerant Johnny Appleseed, he moved about spreading the seeds of goodwill and peace.

Though Dan sought to live simply, his personality was not simple. He was a complex person, "a practical mystic" was the way his friend Kermit Eby put it. There was always a certain mystery about Dan; he wasn't easy to understand. Some said he was stubborn, singleminded, persistent, ruthless in the sense that nothing or nobody could sidetrack him from his course of action if he believed it to be right. A few thought he may have had some traces of desire to grandstand, to be a martyr, yet he had complete disdain for any behavior which called attention to one's self. He often said, "You can get a heap of work done in a day if you don't care who gets the credit for it."

Dan had an aversion to the usual channels of organized effort, yet he had a profound respect for the Church of the Brethren, a denomination of about 180,000 members to which he belonged and within whose insitutions he worked during most of his career. Despite his anti-institutional bias, evident when he refused to accept an honor from his alma mater, Manchester College (a Church of the Brethren college in Indiana) and his choice not to be ordained as a minister, he still worked through church organizations all his life in the interest of youth, peace, and an interfaith, self-help project.

His life reflected his ancestral heritage, the culture which surrounded him, the lives which influenced him, the times in which he lived, and his constant pursuit to better himself, others, and even the world. The goals he set for himself and for others seemed impossible to attain.

But Dan was human. He had great ideas, but he could not

always implement the ideal in his own life. He had faults and foibles. To deny these and picture him as a saint would be to decrease the credibility of his greatness.

While Dan's life may have been enigmatic, he was a brilliant, creative, innovative person, highly educated with an active, alert interest in observing how events in history—economic, political, cultural, spiritual—had shaped and were still shaping the world in which he lived. He was a thinker, a social innovator, and a seer who gathered around him great persons and books to aid in his interpretation of the effects that various movements were having and would have on society.

Some writers have suggested that from time to time a rare individual is born who has capacities and abilities which surpass those of most people. While all of us can see, some are more sensitive, can see more keenly. A true artist observes what many of us fail to note. A perceptive thinker asks questions beyond the usual. The visionary dreams the impossible. Such persons, these writers maintain, not only have superior abilities and capabilities—mental, spiritual, or an innate intuitiveness—but many have had a vision, a flash of insight, or an acute awareness that comes to them around the age of thirty. Most of them spend the remainder of their lives trying to interpret to others what had been made clear to them in that experience.

Dan's insatiable desire to seek further insights and skills to gain more knowledge, and to promote humanitarian activities—the peace movement, the development of human potentialities, volunteer programs, and a self-help project—all these ideas had to be implanted or rooted somewhere. His constant search for truth, his excessive reading, his extensive travel, his mania for probing the thoughts of a wide circle of acquaintances with varied interests, and his art of synthesizing his experiences into some new interpretation and resultant activity seem superior and almost uncanny in perception.

One inkling that Dan might have had an experience which colored and conditioned the balance of his life is found in a letter dated April 29, 1928: "I know what hell is, as I once spent some time in that territory; and I have come out of it, and I know what a difference that makes. If I can actually help anybody to get a better grip on himself, and see a little farther, and struggle more hopefully toward the life that the Master brought, I want to do it. . . . "

It was in the summer of 1916, as a ranger in Snoqualmie Forest in the Cascade Mountains of Washington, that Dan reached the crossroads in his life. He had received an attractive offer to go into a partnership in a business endeavor. Yet Dan felt a strong pull toward the call of his home church—the Pleasant Hill, Ohio, Church of the Brethren—to become a minister. That summer, spent alone, he weighed the pros and cons of the question, "Shall I go into business or shall I serve the church full time?" The church it shall be, he vowed, not as a minister but as a layman. The decision was reached, the direction was set, the course was charted—and "things have never looked the same since."

Dan's commitment to Jesus Christ and the church, with the decision to be baptized at about twelve years of age, remained a guiding force throughout his life. He was deeply committed to Jesus Christ, not as a theological proposition, but as one to be obeyed. He took the life and teachings of Jesus seriously. In his moderator's address at the denomination's 1966 Annual Conference, Dan stressed as the top priority for the Christian the seeking of "the mind of Christ."

"So far as I know, Christ never asked anybody to explain him intellectually. Nor did he ever ask anybody to worship him," said the lay moderator. "Theology and worship patterns are important but not fundamental. Obedience is."

Did he take obedience too seriously? Was the burden almost too great at times? A poem written by Dan which appeared in *The Christian Century,* June 18, 1947 was entitled simply, "Cross."

> *Lovely little symbol on a long lapel*
> *Or dangling from a golden chain about the neck.*
> *Or maybe bigger, bolder, burnished—on a stand.*
> *Improper art, in more than three ways wrong.*
> *Wrong sizes: the cross is bigger than a well-fed man,*
> *And heavy, more than one can carry all alone.*

Wrong places: the cross is rightly worn upon the back.
Wrong finish: the cross is rough, with ugly splinters all
    along.

Later, in a poem, printed in *Messenger,* a Church of the
Brethren magazine, in 1967, asked "Which Cross?"

Dear Lord, my cross is heavy. The weight of it —
With other things — is bending down my head.
My knees are weak . . . My back and arms are sore.
Do I have to carry it anymore?
Couldn't I just worship yours instead?

2
Education of a Non-conformist

The paradoxes in Dan West's life may have been caused in part by the impact of—and the conflict between—an English Quaker father and a German mother. Dan had a growing respect for his mother, but a growing dislike for the militaristic culture from which she came. His mother was the third of fourteen children, the daughter of an authoritarian father. Obedience was the most important thing in her life, and as a result she did not learn self-respect until late in life. Dan's father was quite the opposite. He was an optimist with definite ideas about the dignity of human life and the freedom of individual conscience. He was not awed by authority and often questioned those decisions which differed from his. Dan's young mind sensed the conflict between these two ideologies: one that called for harmony with things as they were (obedience) or one that required rebellion against the war-centered World War I (disobedience).

The Church of the Brethren was equally confusing in its witness concerning the conditions of the world at that time. Though the denomination's Annual Meeting in June, 1916, officially reaffirmed its stand for peace and urged young men to seek exemption from military service, the Brethren in general were not nearly as united in actual practice as their resolutions indicated. The tension between beliefs and actual practice made it difficult for young men to make a decision. It was in this milieu of conflicting thought that Dan had to make his choice.

Since his father had died in 1916, the advice given Dan as he left for the army came from his mother, "When you get in the army, Dan, mind what your superior officers say." These words were unsettling to a twenty-three-year old who had begun to espouse pacifism, and they may have helped to further solidify his basic decision.

Dan's whole struggle, from his induction on May 10, 1917, until his discharge, was to answer the question of "How far can I go?" With some hesitation he decided he could train, he could carry a mess kit, he could even salute. Since he had filled out Form 1008 (for conscientious objectors) he assumed he would receive noncombatant status. But he was wrong. When it came to the showdown: "Anyone here who objects to fighting for the cause of the Allies?" Dan replied "Yes." A talk with the sergeant, Dan thought, had cleared up the matter of his status, but when his name appeared on the list of transfers to the 39th machine gun battalion, Dan stepped forward and said he could not do it. Cursed and taunted by officers, Dan suddenly decided he would go instead to Leavenworth Prison, a decision that seemed to give him peace of mind. "I could stop thinking and go to jail" was a sentence Dan understood well when he read it some time later in a book written by a conscientious objector.

Dan was not sent to prison, nor did he practice on machine guns. His expertise in persuasion and his high score on the Army Alpha Test may have been to his advantage. Dan had no trouble with the military until a young lieutenant held up his application for discharge. With his father's determination, Dan decided to see the general that day—or else. The discharge from Camp Chillicothe, Ohio, came through, and Dan was free! On that day, at the age of twenty-five, Dan West felt he had attained his full self-respect.

With maturity, Dan began to rediscover his heritage—the melding of two almost opposite poles of thought and behavior.

His father, Landon, had been an itinerant preacher, tall and slender, who chose to have his family live on a farm though he was not a farmer at heart. Hitching his horse to the buggy he would be off in his feverish endeavors to help the black Brethren have a better chance in life and to improve the plight of the poverty-stricken in the hills of Southern Ohio and Kentucky. Quoting the Bible came easily for Dan's father, a biblical scholar who used the scriptures freely to denounce all evil.

Born in Adams County, Ohio, in 1841, Landon West as a youth was an ardent student of nature and the Bible. Among his several published books and pamphlets was the book, "Eden's Land and Garden," an explanation of his theory concerning the location of the original Garden of Eden in Adams County. His theory was based on the scriptural interpretation and the Serpent Mound effigy located only a few miles from where he was born. "Close Communion or, Plea for the Dunker People in Two Parts," was published in 1880. The Brethren, often referred to as Dunkers or Dunkards (from the German word *dunken,* to dip), practice trine immersion and celebrate the Lord's Supper with a fellowship meal, feet washing, and communion.

While working among the blacks, West met Samuel Weir, a freed slave who had come to Ohio from Virginia in 1843. Weir found a friend in Landon West, and in 1881 Landon assisted in conducting a love feast at which Sam was ordained as the first black Brethren elder. In 1884, West published a tract called, "The Life of Elder Samuel Weir (a Colored Brother)." It was widely circulated and went through numerous printings with at least 20,000 copies distributed by the tenth edition in 1909. Since Landon's health was poor and his finances limited, he solicited help from the churches in Southern Ohio to print his "Weir" pamphlet, the cost of which was less than one cent per copy.

Elder Landon West, ordained in 1880, was married twice and fathered eight children. To Landon and Barbara Landis West, his second wife, were born five children—Mary, Martha, Susie, Samuel, and Daniel, who was born December 31, 1893, when his father was fifty-four years old. Since Landon did much traveling, it was Barbara who made the day-by-day decisions, saw that the fences were mended, and provided the stability for the family. Tall and poised she worked around the home with the strings of her prayer veil hanging untied, framing her delicate and sensitive face. One neighbor speaks of her "gentle, gracious heart," recalling that on each of her birthdays "Grandma West" brought her two perfect summer Rambo apples from the large tree which grew on the West farm. Well up in years and unable to attend the welcoming shower for the new pastor and his bride, Barbara made them a full-sized quilt of one-inch blocks, all cut, pieced, and quilted by Barbara herself.

The family homestead was old and staunch, as was the Sugar Grove Church (later to become Camp Sugar Grove) around the bend in the road from the West farm. The mill, east and around a curve, was downhill toward the Stillwater River. Highly respected and loved, the family lived for many years in the Pleasant Hill community in Miami County about twenty miles north of Dayton, Ohio.

As the two West boys grew older, Barbara depended more and more upon Sam, the eldest of the two sons. It was Sam who later dropped out of high school to manage the farm for Barbara. Dan was interested in education, travel, and music. He was willing to work if it didn't interfere with his reading or his trips. Though the boys were quite different in temperament and interest, they were close companions.

Dan's mother died in January, 1933, after his marriage in October of the previous year. Dan was very fond of his mother who was always supportive and proud of her youngest son. He spoke often and admiringly of her, sometimes making his wife wonder if she quite measured up to the high esteem and regard that her husband had for his mother.

The three girls in the West family idolized their baby brother. His wishes were their wishes. He was cute, clever, and precocious. He was adored and protected, especially by Mary, his oldest sister who was about twenty years his senior. This doting, this overprotective attitude by his sister may have given Dan an unrealistic start in life.

A bookworm at an early age, Dan read everything he could get his hands on. Prodding him to do his share of the family tasks meant one had to get his nose out of a book and that wasn't always easy. He continued to read intensively and extensively as he sought to broaden his horizons and satisfy his ever-inquiring mind. Later, when a busy schedule began to limit this pleasure, he had to be selective. It was then that he often quoted Ruskin, "If I read this, I cannot read that."

Though his family expected and assumed that he would seek further education, Dan was not particularly interested in formal classroom learning. However, after graduation from Pleasant Hill High School in 1911, he attended Bethany Bible School (a Church of the Brethren institution in Chicago) for a short winter term in 1912-1913. Peers remember that Dan was the only student who wore a tie. This provoked much discussion in a day when the matter of "dress" was an important issue in the church and ties on men were taboo. (Interestingly, Dan's father, who wore a tie, often had difficulty getting the floor to speak at the Annual Meeting when "dress" was a concern, and the Brethren were beginning to splinter in the 1880s.) When Dan later discarded his tie for a more casual appearance, he was criticized for not wearing a tie and for his informal dress at Annual Conference.

While in Chicago, Dan became "tremendously stirred" by a professor at Lewis Institute. He credited this scholar with stimulating his insatiable appetitie for literature and for the perfecting and fine control of language. Those two years (1913-1914) were well spent in honing and sharpening the communicative skills which served him well throughout his lifetime. On weekends, while attending Lewis Institute, Dan continued to hover around the Bethany campus where he kept in touch with Brethren young people and shared his musical talent singing in various quartets.

Degrees seemed to matter little to Dan, who often referred to them as "scraps of paper." He did, however, go to Manchester College, graduating in 1917 with an A.B. degree. Classmates recall that he was a friendly, sociable person, a tall and handsome young man with a soft, melodious tenor voice. He knew almost everyone among the students.

Dan's personality clashed, however, with that of the president of the college, Otho Winger, who desired to make

Manchester big (300). This bothered Dan, for he suspected "big things." Winger was a pragmatist, an activist. He was vigorous and intense, arriving at decisions quickly. Dan was deliberate, took the long look, and was slow in making decisions. Often Dan felt that Winger based his judgments on what was acceptable to the majority or on expediency. Winger's intense drive nettled Dan.

But philosophy was their happy meeting ground. Winger delighted in Dan's quick and alert mind in his philosophy class. The two respected each other, even if they disagreed. There was more pleasure in that than in dealing with students who didn't have the vaguest idea what philosophy was all about.

Perhaps Winger tended to underrate Dan because he sensed that Dan was critical of him. He may have suspected that at times Dan was right. But Winger felt that Dan made a great contribution to Manchester College and years later he paid special tribute to him.

On campus Dan acquired a reputation as a deep thinker, a good conversationalist, and a most eligible bachelor. Discussions—good, lively ones—were stimulating and entertaining to Dan. Nothing pleased him more than "to match brains" with another or "to pick another's brains." In his senior year Dan roomed with James Clarence Keever. A college roomate can be one of the best or one of the worst things that can happen to a college student. Keever was one of the best things that happened to Dan. He often credited Keever with teaching him how to think.

Dan was from Southern Ohio, Keever from Indiana; both were quite mature as college seniors. "Jiminy" was the way Dan always referred to his roommate though classmates do not recall that anyone else ever called Keever by that nickname. They were both philosophical by nature and stimulated each other's minds. No doubt Dan did most of the talking, Jiminy the listening. It was a natural relationship which was mutually enjoyed. The respect and esteem which Dan held for Keever is indicated in a book Dan wrote in 1938, *The Coming Brotherhood*. The tribute read: "I learned something about the meaning of brotherhood from J. Clarence Keever (Jiminy) my pal in college for two years and for more than nineteen years afterward."

One Sunday after Sunday school, Dan, Keever, and two other college students became involved in a discussion that lasted until the bell rang for the noon meal. In telling about it later Dan recalled with a chuckle, "We began talking about pigs, but when the bell rang we were discussing immortality." Who rang the dinner bell that day is not known. It is doubtful if those four realized the time of day. The large college bell was located in the classroom building adjacent to the men's dormitory. A rope, stretched from the bell to the second story hallway of the dorm, was fastened just outside Dan's room. It was Dan's and Keever's responsibility to pull the rope outside their door and ring the bell at rising time in the morning and at mealtimes. One has to wonder how two college students who enjoyed lengthy and weighty discussions could keep the college schedule "on schedule."

One of Dan's most loved and respected professors was Dr. Vernon F. Schwalm, who later wrote: "My first extended contact (with Dan) came in a European History class at Manchester College. Clarence Keever and Dan West were among those enrolled in the class. Whatever the class may have meant to them, it was a stimulating experience to me— with those two stimulating, curious-minded young men.

"When we got to studying the Reformation—especially the German Reformation—Dan was greatly stimulated if not absorbed by a study of Martin Luther and his opposite, Erasmus. He developed a tremendous interest in the methods of these two men: Martin Luther, with his sledge hammer blows vs many of the evils in the church of his days, and the methods of Erasmus who believed that the evils in the church could be removed through reason, that the pen would accomplish more with less violence. Dan wrote a term paper on this topic. Many term papers make rather dull reading but this one I have not forgotten, even though I am saying this 52 years later."

In his senior year in college Dan wrote an essay which his friends still refer to as "a jewel." It appeared in the 1917 *Aurora,* the college yearbook.

Psa. 119:11—Notes
ALL MEN ARE LIARS

*Why that means me, and it's down there where everybody
can see it, too. I never could stand to have any one call me a
liar, and I'll sit down and writ (sic) to him immediately.
What's the fellow's name? Hm! He doesn't seem to have any.*

*Now, let's see about this. I know a farmer who is a liar.
He sold some fresh eggs once that could almost walk. I heard
of a lawyer once that told two lies. I read of a preacher that
told lies regularly. Somebody evidently told a big bunch of lies
about this war. I wonder if that fellow included women in that.
I caught my roommate a couple of times in a lie. And, yes—
come to think of it, he caught me once or twice, and so did Ma.
I guess that takes in about everybody. I reckon that fellow was
right after all.*

*Let's see again. He says. 'I said in my haste, "All men are
liars." What's the matter? Is he going to take it all back? I
don't care, I don't like to change my mind so often. I've got
some interesting news for the next fellow I meet, and I'll quote
some scripture to him, too.*

—Dan West.

3
New Patterns in
Old Values

Now a college graduate and a public-school teacher, Dan used his vacation periods to seek out outstanding professors, rather than universities or graduate courses. He believed *persons* influenced his thinking and stimulated his mind more than the content of the course. His interest was keen in the development of specific skills and techniques. Postgraduate work included Columbia (spring 1919), Chicago (summer 1920), some additional work at Harvard and Ohio State, and a year at Cornell, where he completed all the work for a master's degree but purposively walked out of town just so he wouldn't have to go through the pomp and circumstance of graduation.

At Columbia University he found the bigness of it all to be repulsive. "I hate big things," he often said, associating an undue evil with anything that hinted of bigness. "New York and Chicago," he declared, "were two of America's biggest mistakes."

Kermit Eby, a friend of Dan's, once wrote in an article: "At Columbia University, where Dan went after his army experience, he discovered 'new patterns in old values.' He came home from Columbia one vacation period and a love feast was announced in his church. For the first time in his life Dan couldn't take the church for granted. He asked himself, 'Should I or shouldn't I go to the love feast? For the first time there was a whether in my mind about church.'

"Dan decided to go, and as is the custom in the love feast, he knelt and washed his neighbor's feet. This time, as he knelt, he was beginning to feel and think through his religion. When that love feast was over, the sin of pride had gone from him. Columbia, and all the kudos attached to Columbia, wasn't quite so important anymore."

All this searching and introspection made Dan acutely aware of the various influences which help to form one's life and attitudes. As pondering over his family heritage had led him in an adventure and discovery of self-understanding and self-respect, so a similar struggle had to be resolved relevant to the culture in which he was to live and serve. In retrospect he discovered something which seemed to surprise him. In an article in *Brethren Life and Thought*, a Church of the Brethren journal, Dan explained, "I had hated (as a small boy and youth) the culture which had produced me. . . . Back in the 1920s, a year at Cornell University gave me a new chance to learn new people and ideas and cultural meanings During that Christmas vacation back home, I spent a weekend at a youth conference in Southern Ohio. Sure, these folks were green, with plenty of lacks and faults—I knew them well enough. But in that short time, I came to feel, 'This is my bunch.' That new feeling lasted all through the rest of the year; and it has grown since then. With it came a better appreciation for the people from other cultures. My own self-respect and respect for them deepened together."

Dan's commitment to the church, made at Snoqualmie, was reaffirmed. His basic concern for the life and spiritual health of the Church of the Brethren, his chosen people, was to be paramount in his life and work.

Though universities and colleges sought his services, Dan fervently believed that a teacher can have more influence on the lives of high-school students than on those who are in college. Following his discharge from the army in 1918, Dan taught at Randolph County high school at Englewood, Ohio, for one year. He was a handsome, inspiring teacher. His hair was beginning to gray a bit, adding a certain distinctiveness to his appearance. Students in his manual-arts class were impressed by Dan's sensitive handling of fine woods, his careful instruction in workmanship, and his patient insistence on good finishing.

In 1920, Dan returned to his high school alma mater, Pleasant Hill, where he taught until 1923. For a while he lived with his mother and two sisters in their home about one and one-half miles from town. Because of the uncertainty of the weather and road conditions, he asked to stay in town at the home of his pastor, J. A. Robinson, during the winter months.

The pastor's home was run on schedule, for Robinson was very methodical about his work in the home and church. This was a bit hard on both Dan and Mrs. Robinson since Dan was seldom on time for meals, a very frustrating experience for a woman who planned to serve her family while the food was still good and hot. However, they devised an agreeable and workable plan—the Robinson family would eat on time and Dan would eat whenever he came home, helping himself to the things Mrs. Robinson had prepared for him. Milk was Dan's number one food; he wanted milk at all his meals. No coffee, pie, cake, or sweets of any kind, and meats in limited amounts. Also included in the care of his body was plenty of exercise and his strong conviction against smoking and alcoholic beverages.

Dan didn't date any girls during this period but he wrote letters to many at the same time, for he was quite popular throughout the area. He was chided by the Robinsons about unwittingly making the girls feel that he was seriously interested in them when in reality he was not.

From the vice-principalship at Pleasant Hill, Dan went to Madison Township High School near Trotwood, Ohio, where he taught for five years and became the principal. Though usually understanding and patient with the students, Dan could be brusque. On one occasion a boy in the school was "kicking up his heels" a bit and was sent to Dan for disciplining. As the interview progressed, the boy grew defiant and threatened to quit school. "I'll just take you up on that," was Dan's curt response.

A natural at teaching, Dan's creative ability in instructing high-school students at Trotwood was tested. The textbook in biology lacked practical ideas, and a small budget made it impossible to buy materials. Using the ordinary things around him, such as incubating an egg and watching it hatch in the classroom, Dan devised an effective teaching technique which was ahead of his time. This searching for ideas in the environment surrounding him intensified his concern for the conservation of natural resources, long before it was a popular subject of discussion and concern.

While at Trotwood, Dan and his roommate shared a house with a young married couple. The four of them had many friendly discussions and arguments over the articles which appeared in *The Gospel Messenger,* the Church of the Brethren weekly, and *The Nation,* relating to current events and problems. A long series of articles in *The Christian Century* on the causes of war provoked much debate. Dan was challenged regarding the peace stance of his church. Brethren were biblical in their objection to war, his fellow boarders agreed, but the Brethren were not much interested in the "good society" here and now. The others believed that if peace were to become a reality, the nation should be changed and reorganized by building a society of justice, equality, and equity; by restraining power, wealth, and the corporations; and by challenging the establishment rather than by passive conscientious objection. But Dan insisted that the life of the Spirit was the better way.

In the later years of his school teaching, Dan and a former biology student, by now a teacher himself, discussed the theory of evolution. They concurred on that subject but disagreed on the ideas being espoused by Margaret Sanger. Dan simply could not accept her view of limiting the family through the use of contraceptives. Dan was aware of the changing mores and the new ideas concerning marriage and family. While he was intensely interested in learning what validity there might be in each new concept, the then new and shocking proposals of Judge Lindsay, an early proponent of trial marriages, caused much questioning on Dan's part. He found the idea to be unacceptable.

Though Dan tended to be a loner among his fellow teachers, he was admired and respected by his students at school. To the teen-agers at Sunday school he was a hero. His creative mind and his use of vivid imagery made the characters in the Bible come alive for the students. His skills in leading discussions made the sessions lively and exciting.

Sensitive to the talents, potentialities, and needs of a few special youth, Dan arranged for them to accompany him on trips to church gatherings, to conferences in other states, and to camps. He encouraged them to use their skills, helped them to evaluate their own attitudes and values, wrote letters to keep in touch, and later helped to send some of them for additional training and experience in the United States and abroad. Such opportunities were broadening and valuable to persons whose lives thus far had been spent largely in their home communities. Dan's impact on the lives of these youth was immeasurable and can be attested to by their contributions to the church and society through the years.

Dan was an "original," a unique personality who left strong impressions and influences on those whose lives he touched, especially the idealistic and sensitive young people of the church. His insistent and probing questions forced them to face their own beliefs. He was always sorting through assumptions and cliches in order to arrive at the truth. This was, and continued to be, his mode of learning.

During the period of the early 20s, Dan emphasized the worth of personality and the integration (or wholeness) of personality. He frequently used the illustration of the way people consider others as they jostle around in a crowd—how little attention or value they give each individual in those crowds. Dan suggested that each individual one meets is a personality (personality being something a person *is,* not *has*) but in the rush that person becomes just another obstacle to get around. This marked the beginning of Dan's reference to "the little people" whose cause he championed with never-ending effort. The concept of human worth, the recognition and acceptance of individual differences, and the development of God-given potentialities were ideas which Dan stressed over and over again.

Integration of personality—the focusing of energies, attention, and resources on whatever was decided to be of supreme value to the person—was a frustrating annoyance as well as a stimulating challenge to one of Dan's late-adolescent friends. Once he and Dan were sitting in a church balcony listening to an evangelist drone on and on about salvation. The young man grew restless and finally passed a note to Dan. "Salvation, salvation; what is that man talking about?" Dan sat gazing at the ceiling for a while, then wrote back, "When the man says salvation, let's fit in integration and see where we come out."

On another occasion, Dan's keen and sensitive insight provoked some reflection in the minds of those around him. One November a carload of instructors went to the annual teachers' convention at Columbus. With a half day left after the meetings had ended, the group decided to take a conducted tour of the penitentiary. After the tour, Dan drew a verbal picture of a dense crowd of people laboring up a narrow hill-road. "The people who get in here," he said thoughtfully, "are those who get too far ahead or lag too far behind or stray too far to one side." Then he added a sobering observation, "They look just like you and me; I guess the difference is in the choices they made."

No one could match Dan's facility for apt quotations. He read intensively and remembered copiously. He seemed to be able to pull quotations out of his head as a magician pulls rabbits out of a hat. Two of his admirers picked up the habit of quoting and were known to play far into the night a game which they called "Quotations"—two points for the quote, one for the source, and one for the author.

Such antics turned off another friend, who maintained that a thought worth thinking was a thought worth turning into one's own words. "At 23," he commented, "we want to think as deeply as Thoreau at 33; when we come of age we want to speak in language that would have done Shakespeare credit when he died. We are too proud to be our mediocre, undistinguished selves."

Later this same literary critic softened his indictment of Dan's quoting, for he recognized that Dan thought a great deal through quotations. He took the great ideas of others, modified them, or put them together in new combinations so that from his lips came a new viewpoint.

Dan enjoyed the poetry of Robert Frost, but he didn't like all poetry. Two of Edna St. Vincent Millay's poems he hated with a passion: the familiar one that seems to encourage burning one's candle at both ends and another that mockingly celebrates a "shining palace built upon the sand!"

When his friends, in jest, sang out the musical version of *Invictus,* by William Ernest Henley, thanking "whatever gods may be" for an "unconquerable soul," Dan would grumble in protest, "Bull in a china shop!" or "Just a bantam rooster challenging a thunderstorm!"

To those who knew Dan well a flood of memories comes to mind when certain phrases are mentioned: "Let me point that up,"—"Are you sure of that?"—"Check"—"We do well to have regard for the consequences as well as the aims"—"Are you willing to go as a Christian where there is danger, for Christ's sake?" To a youth with a very positive opinion, he would simply ask, "Why?" He would counter a bold statement by saying, "I like my cheese milder than that." "Let's take the offering and count it" might be a remark made to a person who insisted that the group talk about a subject before all in the group had had a chance to list their concerns. A smile would come over Dan's face when persons disagreed. "Now, we've the makin's of an argument," he would say with delight.

Those who were associated with Dan over a period of years may recall quotation after quotation, statement after statement, verse after verse which he indelibly impressed upon their minds through repetition or through the depth of meaning he gave to the expression. "Habit," he quoted, "is man's best friend or his worst enemy." Then he would acknowledge, "The source is that little chapter on 'Peace,' one of the nine 'strings of beads' in the book, *Apples of Gold,* compiled by Jo Petty, 1962."

4
Persons in Process

While he was teaching in Southern Ohio during the 1920s, Dan enjoyed his work with youth, not only in the public school, but also in the church. He began to realize that the young people needed activities which would bring them together socially, create a greater interest and closer ties with the church, and involve them as contributing members. As yet they were only "silent partners" in the work of the church.

In 1923, Dan organized the first district youth cabinet in Southern Ohio. Though district elders frowned on the idea and those who were a bit conservative tried to deter him, Dan's power of persuasion out-maneuvered the elders and the district board. A district youth cabinet was formed with Dan as its first president and J. A. Robinson, the adult advisor. In November of that year Dan organized and directed a district youth chorus for the Christmas conference to be held at his home church, Pleasant Hill. Evidently Dan could be a rather stern taskmaster. One singer remembers a "bawling-out" he gave some of the singers for being late for rehearsal. When Dan insisted that the group learn the songs so they could sing with confidence without a book, one member reminded him that he was directing from an open song book. Dan, somewhat grimly replied, "As director I'm responsible for the whole thing, and I don't dare make mistakes!"

At the winter conference Dan spoke on "Makers of Peace." It was reported that he was as good, if not better, than a college professor who spoke several times during the two-day sessions. At this same conference Dan, regarded by the less progressive persons as pretty far to the left, pushed for a camp similar to Camp Mack (named after Alexander Mack, one of the founders of the Church of the Brethren) which had been established in Indiana that year. This proposal offered another threat to the oldsters in the district who were going through the trauma of adjusting to ladies' hats, short hair for women, and ties for men (all this before the days of wedding rings and jewelry). Yet they gave their approval, without a dissenting vote, to establish a camp at Sugar Grove, using the abandoned church building which had been the church of Dan's parents and was near the West farm.

The Southern Ohio district youth engaged in many kinds of unifying and exciting activities. The chorus, which Dan had organized, toured the district to secure funds for the camp, raising several hundred dollars from the larger churches in the 50-congregation district. The cabinet, under Dan's guidance, went from church to church talking about peace. Out of this came Dan's great movement "One Hundred Dunkers for Peace."

The national leaders of the church were also beginning to sense the need to establish a program for youth. Chauncey Shamberger gave up his dream to go on to graduate study after college when he was persuaded by the General Mission Board of the denomination to accept a position as director of young people's work. Shamberger had spent a year as pastor at a salary of $1,000 a year with no other benefits. At $150 per month, this new job looked good financially, though there was no provision for moving him from Idaho to Elgin, Illinois. Chauncey took the offer as a challenge, and in September, 1920, he assumed his new task at a time when there were no summer camps, no curriculum for youth, and only a few separate organizations for them. Shamberger learned quickly as he studied other denominations looking for programs which he felt would be feasible for Brethren youth and also meet the approval and support of the adults. The response of the youth was overwhelming; adult support was more difficult to obtain.

Summer camping, Shamberger decided, was the logical place to begin on a denominational scale. In 1921, the first summer camp was held at Winona Lake, Indiana. The second year four camps were promoted, the third year the number was doubled. Year after year they grew. By 1930, there was a chain of summer camps from Virginia to California. A youth program and organization began functioning in many local churches as an outgrowth of the enthusiasm generated in the camp experiences.

As the camping program grew, Dan was called upon more and more to give leadership across the country. Early campers remember him in the khaki uniform of World War I—the khaki shirt and pants with "puttees," a cloth strip wrapped around the leg from ankle to knee. To some it seemed rather strange that a person so dedicated to peace would wear those symbols of the army, but such an outfit was not uncommon for outdoor activities.

Dan believed in "big muscle" work. In each camp where he was a leader, he insisted that the campers do some physical labor to improve the camp grounds. At the Sugar Grove Camp the young people waded into the babbling stream that passed the church (where the camp was housed), threw out the limestone from its floor to deepen it, and made a better swimming hole. Paths were also cleared for vesper sites and an area prepared for the council circle. Dan always seemed to find projects which used the physical energies of the campers for improving the camp.

The typical daily schedule for camp began with an early morning worship period followed by breakfast, a series of classes during the forenoon, a forum in mid-afternoon when the entire group assembled for discussion, recreation, vespers, and the final campfire.

A schedule for Dan was a nuisance. Discussions concerning it seemed a waste of time. He had difficulty keeping one when it was set up. If he was talking with a person about a problem, or if the discussion in a group was still lively and participation active, the time of day or night was not a thing of concern to him. When he was involved in such encounters that person or that topic was the most important thing happening. Of course, this played havoc with plans for the meals. The cooks complained that the food got cold if they waited for Dan and his group. The other campers, already around the tables, were hungry and grew restless. The manager suggested that two or three walking in inadvertently during the thanks for the meal seemed inappropriate. Serving as the laision between the cooks and the leaders, one manager, just thinking about the "unschedule" Dan would keep for rising, eating, and retiring, simply heaved a deep sigh and uttered, "Whew!" Perhaps he was recalling days in camp when he mopped the perspiration from his furrowed brow and simply gave up trying to keep Dan punctual.

But the "open forum" was where Dan excelled! He could take a group no matter how heterogeneous and have every last one of them wanting to get into the discussion. That was a valuable asset. Many leaders could lecture and put most of the campers to sleep, but Dan had all the campers on the edge of their seats wanting to be part of the act. It was a gift!

One of Dan's dependable exercises in many open forums was known as "shades of grey." He would pose one situation that was lily white and then one as black as ebony. Working from both directions he would discover intermediate positions which complicated the issue until the situation became "grey." It was then that Dan had the campers really thinking—was it right? was it wrong?

He had the art of making it appear that each group was special, bringing something new to the discussion that he had never heard before. At the beginning it would seem he had not the slightest idea where the discussion would lead, but those who traveled with him felt certain he knew full well where the group would end up. He always defended himself with the belief that the group reached its own valid conclusion with a minimum of direction on his part. Nonetheless, in each camp the "shades of grey" discussions were pretty much the same.

To get discussions started Dan would occasionally ask the group to suggest subjects they would like to consider. Each volunteer would present a subject, make a short statement about its importance to him and to the group. When no more subjects were forthcoming, Dan would take a vote, and the subject would be chosen. No subject was barred; the questions ranged over the entire area of problems confronting youth from sex to the Trinity.

His insistence that all who wanted to speak, or even looked as if they wanted to speak, should be given that chance, helped to make each one feel that he or she had something special to contribute. Dan seemed perfectly willing to listen to those who got off on a tangent or whose contribution was somewhat trivial or repetitious. He would tactfully get the group back on the subject without ever putting any one down. One wonders how a person with his mental keenness could endure hearing the same ideas expressed over and over. But in this way Dan helped many to believe in their own worth, including the slow ones as well as the brilliant. He encouraged persons to develop their own potential in their own way. He helped each group feel that through its combined effort *it* had reached its own conclusions. Dan would have agreed with the ancient Chinese sage (Lao Tse),

A Leader is best
When people hardly know he exists.
Not as good when people proclaim him,
Worse when they despise him.
But of a good leader, who talks little,
When his work is done — his aim fulfilled —
They will say, 'We have done it ourselves.'

Though many camp leaders admired this slow, deliberate, give-everyone-a-chance method of discussion, other leaders were critical. They felt the discussions, when concluded, were too open-ended; youth were seeking answers, and Dan didn't give any. When he would say to a group, "Now you know as much about this as I do; let's think about it for a while," the critics insisted that common sense would tell you this was simply not true.

Some associates felt he manipulated groups unduly, that he was such a master at it that few could detect his strategy unless they were with him for a long period of time. Others countered that some folks want to be manipulated. Is that the fault of the manipula*tor* or the manipula*ted?* Many saw Dan as stimulating them to think, to evaluate, to seek reasons rather than to accept blindly. These persons argued that Dan was against manipulation by anyone and he would have been shocked, genuinely shocked, if someone openly accused him of it. Dan emphasized that we are all *persons in process,* not static or pigeon-holed. Dan, these young people felt, was so alive that he made everyone who knew him value life more.

Dan once spoke of "confusion" as being the second stage of growth at the time when an individual challenged or doubted his own beliefs. One might say, as a youth did in one of Dan's workshops, "I'm against dancing, but *why* am I against it?" It's the *why* that causes the confusion. When three of Dan's staff challenged his camp leadership as being more dictatorial than democratic, Dan admitted that this "criticism was devilishly hard to accept." He couldn't believe this about his own style. As he began to accept this criticism, *he* became confused.

At mealtime, leaders and campers alike relaxed in moments of banter, jokes, and singing. They simply enjoyed being with each other. Though Dan was jolly and enjoyed a good, clean joke, he maintained a sensitivity to inappropriate fun. By quietly raising a question or expressing in a calm way his displeasure with an idea, Dan seemed to stimulate youth to pick up his challenges. A group of campers in Michigan sang "Snowball" (Oh, Mammy, Mammy, tell me about those white folks' chillun/Why do they call me Snowball when Snowball ain't my name?). Instead of berating them for their racist lyrics Dan simply said he wished there were more acceptable words to such a nice tune. The group spent the rest of the week composing a camp song to the tune. Having started the process, Dan refused to have any more to do with it, assuring them that the group was more than adequate to find just the right words.

Though Dan liked the original words which referred to the heavenly chariot in the song, "She'll Be Comin' 'Round the Mountain When She Comes," he abhorred the sound effects which were so popular in the 30s (red pajamas, "hack, hack," etc.). When the campers sang, "She will ride so level and steady when she comes," Dan joined in solidly and with a great deal of dignity.

Outdoor vesper services at sundown provided an introspective experience for campers. Songs sung antiphonally (across a valley) produced the feeling of awe, wonder, and contemplation. Tired from classes and recreational games, the campers experienced God's world of nature as calming, soothing, and inspiring. The sun sinking over the horizon, clouds changing into imaginative shapes, the cricket's chirp, a bird's trill, and the silence of persons in tune with God and with each other gave the feeling that "God's in his heaven; all's right with the world." (Browning). Vespers by a lakeshore could be breathtaking as candles, symbols of each person's life and witness, floated away on the water and were soon lost from sight.

One memorable vesper service was held at an abandoned quarry, a short hike from the Sugar Grove Camp. Dan stationed himself strategically at the juncture of two quarry walls, over which the balance of the campers were dangling their legs. He quietly reached over the edge and pulled a little weed out of a crack. Then he opened his remarks with Tennyson's lines beginning, "Flower in the crannied wall/I pluck you out of the crannies. . . . "

From vespers the campers usually hiked on a narrow path through the trees to the campfire or council circle. Unable to maintain the spell of quietude much longer, the young people began chattering and laughing. Their voices, full of fun and excitement, filtered through the trees giving God's creation new life and vitality, vibrant with youth's suspense of anticipation and excitement at the close of the day.

Something unexpected often did happen at campfire. On one surprise occasion, at Camp Mack in Indiana, it was prearranged that Dan should be given a suitable title. With due ceremony Dan was dubbed "Phis-co-te," presumably an Indian name meaning philosopher, scholar, and teacher.

Around the campfire, seated on logs or blankets, the campers wriggled and squirmed to get in a comfortable position. As they settled in, an enthusiastic, vigorous song leader, Al Brightbill, began with action songs, a few silly little ditties, then a round or two. By this time he had their rapt attention as they watched his every direction. Perhaps "America, the Beautiful" would be next, then "Fairest Lord Jesus," or "This Is My Father's World," ending with the quieting "Dear Lord and Father of mankind, forgive our foolish ways. . . . " A transformation had taken place! The hilarious, disjointed group of thirty minutes ago now sat waiting eagerly for the message.

While the forum periods provided invaluable opportunities for youth to express themselves and to grapple with their problems and doubts, to many Dan was at his best around the campfire. Inez Long describes what so many campers remember: "The red orange light of the campfire threw shadows on the faces of the campers under the trees. It outlined the speaker standing near the center of the circle. Suddenly the fire flashed, tracing sharply in light and shade the profile of a man.

"He spoke in a casual manner, his shirt open loosely at the throat, his sleeves folded back in neat carelessness below the elbow. Bending easily toward the campers as he spoke, he was like a giant willow at the lakeshore leaning toward the well-springs of its life. Even as he spoke to the youth around the campfire, he was learning from them. That speaker, Dan West, has taken the vigor of his youthful audiences to put force into ideas which will grow for many years to come." (from *Brethren Trail Blazers*).

Campers were encouraged to express their commitment to discipleship, but they were never forced. Some campers chose to state their decisions before the group; others opted to do it privately. Some tossed a stick into the fire symbolizing a habit or a hurtful attitude which they wished to eliminate from their lives; others chose to remain seated with their own thoughts. The leaders accepted equally either method of decision-making. Many campers made resolutions there which influenced the direction of their lives.

When the flames of the fire had been reduced to glowing embers, the campers quietly and contemplatively returned to their bunks for a night's sleep. Often, however, one camper would remain, staring pensively into the fire. Dan would sense the youth's need to talk and would linger behind, sometimes talking far into the night.

That his patience in listening, his openness to new ideas, his quiet sympathetic manner influenced thousands of campers is beyond question. Many have not been the same since his life touched theirs. In a sincere tribute to Dan, Chauncey Shamberger reflected, "If the camping movement had done little more than bring a personality like Dan West into the lives of youth, its mission was justified."

5
The Summer
That Became
a Legend

One particular summer has become a legend in Brethren camp history. It was just prior to the time Dan moved to Elgin, Illinois, to succeed Chauncey Shamberger as national director of young people's work. Though all of the leaders involved in this one summer's experience had been traveling to conferences and camps together for a number of years, the summer of 1929 seemed to be special. Chauncey would soon be leaving; Dan would be coming to take his place.

Chauncey, known as "Chief," was the administrator, Dan the discussion leader, Al Brightbill the music leader, and Perry Rohrer the recreation director. These four, dubbed "The Four Horsemen," moved from camp to camp for the lavish salary of $35 per week. They covered almost 7,000 miles in the venerable Studebaker sedan they used each of four summers, 1927-1930. Changing drivers frequently and traveling at night, they once left a camp at New Windsor, Maryland, on Saturday morning and were signing in campers near Palmer Lake, Colorado, on Monday morning!

Some people may have looked upon camping as a vacation but for those who felt the responsibility to make each camp meaningful for each young person it was a strenuous and exacting time. These men who went from camp to camp, week after week, became specialists, and because they were trained for it they carried a heavier load than those leaders who came in from the area and gave only a week or two to a particular camp. But the camaderie and the close association made up for all the headaches and heartaches these itinerant leaders may have had.

Taking turns driving the "Sweet Chariot," the nickname they gave the unreliable vehicle, the Four Horsemen (plus Joe Van Dyke in 1929) usually traveled on Sundays to get to the next camp. An impromptu "Sunday service" evolved as they sang all the songs and hymns they could remember. Al strummed his guitar, though finding rooms for it was a problem with five men and their camp gear crammed together in the old car. In the midst of the songfest Dan enjoyed telling about the black conscientious objector who stepped out of rank and sang a spiritual. His moving story usually called forth more seriousness in their singing as they bounced along day and night on the graveled roads, averaging about 35 miles per hour.

The Sweet Chariot served as a home away from home, a place where all five were together alone once again—joking a bit, poking fun at each other, trying to relax, evaluating the past camps and preparing for the next. The five felt a sense of elation that another camp was over, and yet they were eagerly looking forward to the next one which would be uniquely different from all the others.

Those hours spent together are recalled with fondness by Chauncey and Joe, the two men of the five-member team still living. If something fell flat in a camp they sought the reason for it and tried to avoid a recurrence. If one of them did something that did not appear to be quite right, it was brought out in the open. At one campfire where the visitors were noisy and failed to enter into the spirit of the camp, Chief reprimanded them rather harshly. Later Dan very cautiously told Chauncey that he had overdone it a bit.

Idiosyncracies are magnified and become more irritating when people are together for long periods and in intimate situations together. This group was no exception. They accused Chief of always being at the wheel when they drove into camp—"an impressive introduction inferring that he was boss." His funny stories, they said, weren't funny—"You'd better let somebody else tell the jokes." Al never seemed to have any money. He was fascinated by the old organs often donated to the camps and usually needing repairs. The other four complained that he spent too much of his time fixing them.

Dan inspected kitchens of restaurants and though he sometimes preferred not to eat some places because of what he saw, the other hungry men usually outvoted him. Dan was joshed and teased about all the girl friends, always the prettiest ones, he found interesting in each camp. And was "Come, Ye Disconsolate" the only tune he could play on his violin? But there was a jovial and relaxed side to Dan. He seldom told a joke for humor's sake but his deep, quiet understanding of humor was seen in the twinkle of his eyes. That he was always aware of humorous situations made him a good traveling companion.

Perry, already interested in psychology, reflected on human behavior, sometimes irritating the group a bit. Joe? Joe was quiet but listened and thought a lot. The most unpredictable driver turned out to be Dan because he soon forgot what he was doing as his mind wandered to more important things. Plowing into a car near Columbus, Ohio, Dan, in his straightforward frankness, simply announced, "I hit 'im!"

Some summers prior to 1929, Dan had suggested that it might be helpful if, at the close of the camping season, each person would write the others an evaluation of their strengths and weaknesses. Though the comments were sometimes hard to take, they were given with love and received with acceptance. It was a rather ruthless experience, but through the years each expressed to the others a genuine appreciation for the insights given in these evaluations.

At the final camp of 1929, near Palmer Lake, after all the campers were in bed, the five gathered around the glow that remained of the campfire upon the mountainside. It was quiet as each contemplated the next day's parting. Finally the silence was broken as one suggested, with the others agreeing, that instead of writing the evaluations this time they might, as a group, talk over the comments.

The five had been close enough that frankness was accepted as their basis of understanding. Around the circle each one gave a critique of the others based on the summer's experience. When they came to Dan one suggested that Dan's interest in people might not be as much in the person as in the functioning of his or her brain. Dan was a thinker, they counseled, and he respected people in proportion to their ability to keep up with him. All agreed with the observation. It was a shock to Dan because he felt he had a genuine interest in all persons no matter what their intellectual powers. He suggested that he would spend hours talking with someone who simply needed him. It was easy to see that he had no idea that he could be valuing persons in such a way. Yet the other four thought it was true.

It followed naturally that this same concern was related to Dan's relationship with the opposite sex. Four members of the team were married; Dan wasn't. They told him that at 36 he should be marrying. He had formed the habit, they said, of allowing some of the most beautiful and intellectual women all over the country to think he was in love with them. The group believed that he thought of them, not as lovers, but minds. It was time for him to target in on some lovely person whose mind was good and who also had a heart. They assured Dan that the criticism of certain aspects of his personality was quite insignificant to the deep respect and love they all had for him.

Because of the long and intimate friendship which existed among the team members Dan was willing to take seriously what they urged.

After reading a letter he had written to his mother during that memorable summer of '29, Joe Van Dyke summarized his observations. "I wrote that I had the most fun with Perry and I liked Chief best. I said nothing about Dan in that letter. I think I know why I didn't try to label how I felt about Dan. I liked Dan so much, but I never felt at ease with him as I did with the others. I never felt I came up to his expectations of me. Dan had a sense of humor, but I never kidded him, never had fun at his expense. I think I was sort of awed. I know he didn't want to create awe in anyone, but I always felt a distance. He seemed to be almost another order of being."

What effect did these camp leaders have on the campers? To wash dishes with Dan, to eat and laugh together at the same table with Al, to go swimming in Winona Lake with Chauncey, to build a campfire with Perry, or to rub shoulders with other church leaders meant much to the young campers. Here they saw persons of leadership who were willing to be one with them. These were persons who believed in youth and proceeded on the basis that youth could be trusted for their inherent goodness, rather than building fences about them to save them from their badness and from the badness of the world. The young people were delighted with the camps and flocked to them in great numbers.

Yet some members of the churches were not as happy with the camping program as were the young people. Al Brightbill once overheard Dan being lashed with ugly words by a church leader "for helping our youth go to the dogs." But Dan in his characteristic way answered with soft words of empathy and with an understanding of the generation gap—even then when the older generation had the long hair and beards.

Dan had a strategy that worked at Camp Bethel in Virginia. One district in that area which was not enthusiastic about camps for youth sent a few of its board members to see what was going on. Dan suggested that the elders from the board and the campers play baseball during the recreation period. The visitors should do the batting; the young campers would run the bases for them. It was amazing how the visitors' attitudes changed when they participated with the youth and became part of the group. Discussions about camp and the youth program in that district seemed to change from then on.

In spite of the initial objections, camping, now as then, continues to captivate and challenge the imaginations of youth for commitment to and service in the church.

6

Push Them Out
of the Nest

Soon after Dan became national director of young people's work in 1930, he wrote an article in *The Gospel Messenger,* June 13, 1931. Characteristically he began by raising a question: "Shall we try to keep our young people safe in the nest, making them believe exactly as we do? or shall we do as the eagles—push them out of the nest?

Realizing the vitality of youth, he suggested that this abundant energy needed to be guided but, he cautioned, their activities must be their own. "They want to be persons, not things," he wrote, "and we do well to learn to respect those whom we would guide to a more abundant life. If we urge them out in an adventure of their own, in what direction should it be?" he challenged. In the article the five programs which he advocated and for which he worked most of his life are punched out in 1, 2, 3 order.

1. Recreational life. Rather than spend energy fighting commercial entertainment, suppose the young people were urged to *create* a recreational program that would give life and not destroy it. There should be at least one young person in every church district who would serve as a recreational expert.

2. Home life. With the development of the so-called secular life there is no certainty that all the present homes are built upon a rock. Neither can the homes the youth are establishing be depended upon as secure. There should be a program in every church to prepare youth for homes of the future.

3. Income. In the midst of the present depression (1931) and the scramble for more money, it was a good time to ask, "Am I my brother's keeper?" Can one make money off his brothers and sisters and love them at the same time? If the young people would turn away from the competitive order in which they live, and try to build their lives on the creative and sharing motives rather than on the profit motive, would their parents stand for such "foolishness?"

4. Religious life. While some of the young people are trying to substitute the new science for an old faith, others were becoming impatient with the lack of religious fervor, and were being drawn toward high emotional excitement and religious "whoopee." Dan wondered how the fearless hunting after truth could be combined with an eager but humble reaching toward God in new ways that would stabilize the soul and give abundant life?

5. Peace on earth. "When I see so much that the war makers are doing and so little that the peacemakers are doing, I wonder why the difference. . . . Find me one hundred Dunkers between the ages of twenty-one and thirty who will give as much for peace as a soldier gives for war, and we will change the thinking of Congress in three years' time. Would you like to push your young people in that direction?" he asked.

His concluding paragraph: "Maybe you don't like these suggestions. All right. Make up some that you do like, or ask your young people to help do it. Then 'push them out of the nest.' Nothing binds people closer than fellowship in a great adventure. And nothing without adventure will keep our youth in the church. The Church of the Brethren ought to be, not a circumference, but a center for her youth."

One of Dan's overriding objectives during the six years he was director of young people's work was to bring about changes in persons so they could and would be challenged to serve the church effectively. The personal life change, he felt, came with an understanding of self, a suitable solution to one's inner problems, and a satisfying relationship with God and with associates.

Dan continued to spot young persons in whom he saw great potential and good leadership possibilities. In the fall of 1929, Ben Stoner, a young man from Indiana, was encouraged to spend a year in Europe. Dan arranged for Stoner to go to Geneva, Switzerland, and either contributed $1,200 himself or saw that Ben received enough to make the trip. Ben enrolled for courses in the Institute of International Relations in Geneva, a branch of the University of Chicago, and later went to Hanover, Germany, to observe the Hitler Youth Movement. Upon returning from Europe, Stoner spent several summers in Brethren youth camps sharing his experiences with the young campers, emphasizing the need for understanding and the hope for peace on earth, Dan's dream.

In 1931 Dan suggested to Robert Noffsinger and J. Harmon "Si" Bjorklund that a trip to Mexico might be more important than their work as seniors at Manchester College. They attended the first Protestant Youth Camp in Mexico held in the shadow of Mt. Popocatepetl. Dan gave each of them $200, slightly less than one-half the cost of the trip. While Dan had no great wealth, he would "lend" money with the suggestion that they pass it on in some like manner when they were financially able. He never required a note for he felt keenly about helping people without any direct repayment.

The trip for Noffsinger and Bjorklund was a part of Dan's broader vision of the youth of the world becoming intimately acquainted with the customs, habits, and social and spiritual ideals of each other. In so doing he felt that war between peoples would be "squeezed out of the picture."

Robert Tully was fresh out of college and unable to find a job in the depression year of 1931. While he was not at the conference which outlined the plans, he responded to an invitation in *Our Young People*, a Church of the Brethren youth paper, to assist as a volunteer in one of the programs adopted at the first youth meeting held in conjunction with the denomination's Annual Conference. The youth had selected peace and recreation as their emphases for the next ten years. Bob's offer to help resulted in an invitation to spend two weeks in Elgin studying recreation and the Church of the Brethren. One of Dan's basic premises, a statement many heard him repeat time and time again, was an ancient recipe for bear stew: "If you want bear stew, you must first get the bear!" Bob was to be the "bear" in the "soup" of recreation.

Since Dan had been much impressed by a Mormon leader's evaluation of their nine-year church-centered recreation program—"It has saved our youth for our church"—Bob, with his wife, visited for two weeks at the headquarters of the Church of Jesus Christ of Latter-Day Saints at Salt Lake City, studying their programs. As a result of this training, Bob spent five summers in camps and conferences leading recreation for youth. Pulling into Camp Harmony in Pennsylvania one summer, Dan and Bob observed a pillow fight in progress. "Bob," said Dan with a grin, "there's your challenge. Get in there and get those kids started in some positive recreation!" Dan's emphasis and preparation for recreational leadership resulted in the formation of the Recreation Fellowship with recreation workshops and laboratory schools conducted throughout the church.

Dan helped to make it possible for Kermit Eby, a young Brethren school teacher in Ann Arbor, Michigan to travel to Japan in 1933. When Eby returned to America he worked dilligently to try to bring about a better understanding between the people of the United States and the people of Japan. Through such interaction Dan hoped to remove the international tensions that were leading to World War II. Eby later became an influential labor leader.

Bjorklund, with Dan's nudge, went to England in 1936 to further better relationships with the British. In a geography class at a boys' school the students shot questions to Si as fast as he could answer them for one hour. He was chagrined to find their ideas about America vague and incorrect, ideas which had been colored by sensational newspaper stories.

Visiting college students to keep them in touch with the church was another of Dan's priorities. He befriended James

Erbaugh in his lonely years in school at Chicago, even loaning him $200 to finish his education. Dan stopped off to visit Paul Robinson (Dan's former pastor's son), the only Brethren student at Princeton Theological Seminary at that time. Paul gathered some of the other fellows, most of them Presbyterians, to meet with Dan. It was in the fall of 1938 when the war clouds were gathering in Europe. Dan had returned from relief work in war-torn Spain and was conceiving what later developed as the Heifer Project. The men at Princeton were greatly impressed with Dan. Some thought he was unreal because he had radical ideas about peace and self-defense. He talked of nonviolence at a time when not to defend one's self was considered insane. While many of the students could not accept his perspective, many were influenced by what he said. His gentleness, sincerity, and consistency carried their own message. A few said that the kind of naive outlook on life which they heard from Dan marked him simply as a visionary who was out of touch with reality. Others felt that he was the first person they had heard in those troubled times who made any sense.

Did Dan, who had such a keen interest in recreation—in the re-creating of one's body, mind, and soul—take enough time out for himself to play and relax? He gave the impression that there was often too much to be done. He did not really seem capable of just relaxing. Bouts with shingles proved annoying to him, for they limited his activities. Fortunately, he was able to recoup his strength with catnaps on a depot bench, on a church pew, or leaning against a tree at camp. Such brief periods of rest seemed to refresh him sufficiently to keep up the pace he endured. Sleep may have come easily because he was "doing his thing" for the church and he was doing it the best he knew how.

In the early 30s Dan, who believed that leadership was most effectively developed through the use of small groups, initiated what was called the "hilltop" movement. In an account of a "hilltop" in Iowa the quotation, "A rough place, as rough as life itself," preceded the description of the movement: "The development of effective leadership for youth in the Church of the Brethren . . . through honest searching for truth in the big problems of modern life, group criticism of everyone, creative dreaming, personal commitment to creative religious work, steady and quiet work where they are . . . sharing with one another—an adventure toward transforming the Church of the Brethren into a great spiritual power for the Kingdom of God."

Groups of not more than twenty youth and leaders met in a casual, free atmosphere over a weekend, discussing and searching together. The membership crossed all age lines, sex lines, and color lines. Most came from Brethren backgrounds but not all. Learning the real meaning of acceptance—of oneself and of others—and the creative handling of conflict were areas which were especially emphasized.

Toward the end of the period together any person in the group who wished—no one was forced—could volunteer to "take the chair," to become the subject of attention, even criticism, while other members attempted to give that person insights, both positive and negative, leading to a better self-understanding. "Speak the truth in love" was the admonition given prior to any evaluation.

At the second "hilltop" meeting, held June 19-22, 1933, Dan "took the chair." The following comments were recorded in a booklet sent to all the participating "hilltoppers" in that group: Dan should spend more time in school at a university, develop a better time consciousness, spend more time writing, give his own opinion when asked for, and share his abilities with young folks outside the Brethren group.

One psychologist felt the "hilltop" movement was more hurtful than beneficial. Another said, "It scared the very bejabers out of me and still does because, as in this case, the cult of the amateur is too often overglorified." But there are leaders in the church today who point to the "hilltop" experience as the turning point in their lives, more helpful than similar group sessions subsequently sponsored by seminaries or universities. In a day of group therapy and sensitivity training this technique does not seem unique, but for that time it was new and revolutionary.

7
Building a Conscience for Peace

Dan continued his travels throughout the Church of the Brethren emphasizing his ceaseless belief and hope that peace in the world was viable. Serving on various study and action committees, he dreamed of further contacts and ways to involve others in carrying out his conviction that peace could, and would, come on earth.

With the formation of a Peace Committee in 1928 as part of the national Board of Christian Education of the Church of the Brethren, youth peace contests and peace caravans, composed of college students who traveled during the summer in the interest of peace, were sponsored and supported. These activities increased the desire of the youth of the church for a more definite program of peacemaking. This found expression in a group already referred to as "One Hundred Dunkers for Peace." Formed in 1932, it was Dan's organization of young people who were looking for the "moral equivalent of war," a phrase Dan used often. Dan was trying to keep within the church-fold young students who (1) were vitally interested in peace, (2) would need support against the pressure of public opinion in a time of national crisis, and (3) had become increasingly disgusted with the apparent impossibility of getting enough action through established channels.

Volunteer service for the cause of peace was another movement which appealed to youth. Summer work camps were initiated by the American Friends Service Committee. In 1934 the AFSC wrote to Dan asking him to suggest names of young people who would help in the resettlement of coal miners on farms in Pennsylvania. Dan summed up such a project as "an attempt to achieve social justice without violence and to give training to those who may become guides of peace activities in case war cannot be prevented."

With many persons working to build a peace conscience among the Brethren, there was sufficient concern by 1935 about the problem of conscientious objectors that a committee, with Dan as a member, was designated to provide legal counsel for the COs. The next year the committee gave guidance to potential draftees by listing types of service considered consistent with the historic peace position of the church. In addition the committee suggested specific ways in which all members of the denomination could show their convictions against war-related activities.

As in 1916 the statements made by the church were far ahead of its members. Dan was caught in this ambiguity and was also hindered in his work by personnel changes in boards and committees over a twenty-year period. Though there had been a wide distribution of peace literature the young people had not been sufficiently involved in discussions where points of view were challenged and changed. Thus the majority of the youth were not as effectively reached as Dan had hoped.

Early in 1936 the American Friends Service Committee formed a group called the Emergency Peace Campaign (EPC). They asked the Church of the Brethren to release Dan West for one year to work with young people of all denominations in the interest of peace. He visited campus after campus, locating outstanding students who would be trained and sent out in peace caravan work during the summer of 1936. The response was overwhelming. More than five hundred youth responded from many denominations across the country. So many volunteered that only about one half could be used. The EPC represented the most wholehearted support the Brethren had ever given to a cooperative program of action for peace.

Meanwhile the One Hundred Dunkers for Peace was becoming a more cohesive group. By their own description, they were "members of a new generation of young Dunkards who wanted to save the world, not through withdrawal but through permeating and leavening the social group, and through attacking the problems of the modern world with intelligence and direction." They didn't condemn the past as much as they felt forced to condemn themselves if they slavishly followed the patterns of the past instead of creating new techniques that could work in the present.

One June 1, 1937, the first issue of *Brethren Action,* an unofficial mimeographed magazine, was published with a subscription of $1.00 per year. It was designed to keep the Hundred Dunkers and other like-minded Brethren informed about the activities of the group and to serve as a medium for exchanging ideas. In typical Dan West style, its first editorial asked:

"What things in our Dunker heritage are worth conserving in an age of high-powered automobiles, scientific advance, and the urbanization of rural life?

"Should the Church continue its former isolation from the 'world' and attempt to build up rural oases in which the customs, patterns of living, and *weltanschauung* shall be relatively little influenced by those of the world outside? Would it be possible for it to do so if it wanted to? Can the principles and practices of the Church of the Brethren be made universal? How can we help to make this a better world in which to live?

"What should we do toward the elimination of war, racial discrimination, and economic justice? What should young married people strive for—an income that will enable them to live in comparative luxury and to go in for elite society?"

Hopefully, the paper was to help give answers which many young idealists in the Church of the Brethren were groping to find to the social problems of the day.

A report of a meeting of the Hundred Dunkers for Peace,

held in Dayton, Ohio, on May 22, 1937, revealed some interesting and significant statements made by Dan: "I am impressed how little people do for peace," and "When I must choose between citizenship and Christianity, I will take the latter." To encourage the small group, banded together in the interest of peace, Dan urged them to continue their peacemaking work in all of its facets. "I will enjoy my trip to Spain in September if I know something is going on in America!"

8
Husband and Father

Did Dan West, a popular and eligible bachelor of over thirty-five, have no other interests than all his "church business"? His qualities of serenity, intelligence, and handsomeness were attractive characteristics. In the office where he worked and in the churches he visited many young women were tempted to look at him romantically, even though he gave them little encouragement.

Though Dan and Lucille Sherck had seen each other before, it was at the Union Center Church of the Brethren (Indiana) that something very personal and spiritual awakened between them. Lucille was making a speech, "The Charm of the Impossible." Dan was in the audience. He listened intently. She spoke forcefully as one who was stimulated by the responsiveness of her listeners.

On December 12, 1931, this charming and attractive woman arrived at the denomination's headquarters to work in the Missionary Education Department. When Dan began to look with favor on Lucille Sherck, twelve years his junior, several well-meaning women cautioned, "Be careful, Lucy, you'll get hurt!"

Dan's favorite toast had been, "Here's to those who wear old clothes and have no wives to mend them." It now began to look as if he was reconsidering the last part. Had Dan found the "lovely person whose mind was good and who also had a heart" as the five friends had advised as they sat around the dying campfire near Palmer Lake in 1929?

Lucille came from a large family of six brothers and two sisters, living most of her life on a farm north of Middlebury, Indiana. A graduate of Shipshewana High School, determined to get a college education, Lucille took part of her school work between stints of teaching and during the summers, graduating from Manchester College in 1930. Her first experience in teaching was in a rural area at the Saylor School near LaGrange, Indiana—all eight grades with thirty-six children. Lucille enjoyed her pupils and teaching.

The relationship between Dan and Lucille deepened. When they became engaged, Lucille knew Dan would be gone much of the time. She was aware of his dedication to the church and his intense interest in ideas, learning, travel, and people, but she felt the cost was not too great when compared to other young men whose goals were less important and less enduring.

On October 8, 1932, Daniel West and Lucille Sherck were married in the Middlebury Church of the Brethren with Edward Frantz, editor of *The Gospel Messenger,* officiating. Dan, some friends thought, may have married because he believed in the family. He felt and spoke of the family as the base of a good life. But letters between the two showed a deep devoted love for each other, some in the form of poetry by Dan. The covenant made on that wedding day was kept through times of joy and times of tears.

Though she did not marry Dan just to become "Mrs. Dan West," Lucille's life was no doubt filled with wider, deeper, richer, and more varied experiences because she was his wife. But she added much to Dan's life, too, for she gave him something of beauty in the subtleties of daily living, and an invaluable influence in tempering his idealism with realism. She helped him greatly in the fulfillment of his dedicated commitment to his calling.

Though expressed in rather subtle ways, it seemed that Dan did not regard women as equals. He expected a great deal of his wife. His absences from home for as much as eight months of a year left the care and rearing of the five children largely up to her. Later the management and supervision of a large farm became a heavy responsibility. His attitude toward women was seen again in his relationship with his daughter, Janet. Her four brothers often felt sympathetic toward her, feeling that their father couldn't understand her simply because she was a girl.

Both Dan and Lucy wanted a big family—4 or 5 (they didn't count on twins) in a time when two was the popular number. Dan was at Camp Harmony in Pennsylvania when he received the message that Lucy, as Dan called her, had fallen on the basement steps. Knowing that she was expecting their first child, Dan hurried home. Joel was born July 21, 1934, while the Wests were living at Elgin, Illinois. The forty-year-old father was overjoyed at the birth of their first son.

Feeling the urge to live closer to the "grass roots" of the church to identify more with people in local churches, Dan made his desire known through an article in *The Gospel Messenger*. The pastor at Ottawa, Kansas, invited the family to become part of that community. The Wests moved there in the fall of 1934, remaining about a year while Dan continued his staff duties.

The next move was to Newville, Pennsylvania in 1935 where Janet was born on August 30, 1936. It was here that Lucy and the two small children lived while Dan served as a relief worker in Spain during the Spanish Civil War.

Upon his return to the states, Dan and Lucy made a deliberate decision to move to a farm for the training they felt country life would afford the children. As the children grew they would learn the laws of nature, of growth, of production of food, of the care of animals, of sharing tasks, burdens, and joys. Soon after their move to a farm near Dunlap, Indiana, six miles northwest of Goshen, the twins, Philip and Lawrence, were born on October 4, 1938. Guess who carried them in his arms to church the first Sunday? Not even the mother had a chance! "It was complete work for me; sheer joy for Dan," laughs Lucy as she tells about it. Born five years later on May 22, was Steven, who often felt the age gap between him and his energetic and hard working older siblings.

The days on the 30-acre Dunlap farm (27 tillable acres,

rest wooded) hold the fondest memories for all the children. It was there they learned to love rural life, the simple life. They enjoyed the beauty of the woods, swinging on the vines, building elaborate tunnels and large dark rooms, high enough to stand up in, with the bales of hay, and packing snow into igloos in the yard during the winter.

Daisy, a big Belgian mare, was lovingly cared for by the children. All five squeezed closely together as they enjoyed with childish delight a ride on her broad back. It was a glorious morning when they discovered that after eleven months Daisy had given birth to a long-eared, black foal. The little boys had witnessed the mating of Daisy and had a special appreciation for Long-ears, her mule offspring. Hitching Daisy to the mud boat, which ordinarily hauled manure and firewood, everyone in the family hopped on, and off to the woods they went with a lot of picnic things. Occasionally, they were joined by Dan's secretary, who also served as a baby-sitter and helper for Lucy.

Living on the farm was fun and exhilarating to the entire family. Perhaps one of the reasons the children felt the strength and joy of rural life so strongly was because Dan often brought friends home after his travels, or he would write and invite them to stay several days. The youngsters caught the guests' excitement as they came to the West's small farm and participated in their family and their animal life.

Dan had a definite life-style which was rooted on the farm and grounded in nature and biology. His understanding of plants and animals, and of the weather, and his open participation with these wild things probably had the most lasting influence on the children. They were impressed by the tender care taken in transplanting cabbages and tomatoes—keeping the roots wet before disturbing them, packing the soil firmly around the newly-moved plants, watering quickly after placing them in the ground, and watching them closely the first few days to make certain they got a good start. It was a kind of ceremony, a ritual, which their father meticulously and lovingly carried out.

On this farm the children caught a deep sense of the drive to achieve. Dan had developed a tremendous compulsion to excel in his endeavors. He passed this attitude on to his children, indirectly perhaps, but they caught the message. In conversations with them he told of the conscious decisions he had made earlier in his life, sorting out pretty much what he had wanted his life to be like. It was a firm commitment to the bettering of society, using many puritanical values and with his family as a testing ground. He was sure that his children would not make the same mistakes that he had made, and that their children would do the same in relation to them. Dan's commitment to improving society required very serious thinking, so work came first in the morning, play in the afternoon. To a degree he wanted to remove much of the immaturity of childhood and replace it with quick growth among his children. Dan was totally committed to his value system.

At home as well as in camps, Dan was an advocate of "big muscle" work. Ironically, with the family it was in an area of life he knew little about, farming. Dan was raised on a farm, but he lacked the rough and ready, do-it-yourself attitude that an earnest farmer must have. Farming was his hobby and setting, but his commitment was to a better world — to the poor and unfortunate. While Dan did do some farm work he always looked quite dignified behind a plow. He seldom worked up a good sweat doing tasks on the farm. His young children loved watching their neighbor men because they would sweat, swear, and slap their horses, indications to them that that was work! Dan *did* instill in his children the attitude of hard work, though he seldom got intensely involved in it himself.

Lucy was also responsible for the pressure. When there was a task to be done, she pitched in to get it finished. She worked right along with the boys. One June morning, striding toward a gunny sack on the fence, she cranked the hand seeder, sowing alfalfa on the hill field before driving the children to the church's Annual Conference to join their father. One of the boys recalls his father's caution, "Don't overdo," for he seemed to fear heavy work himself; Lucy did not.

This sense of drive invaded many areas of their life. While both Dan and Lucy were conveying their ideas to work hard, to achieve, to excel, the children seem to feel that it was Dan who implanted it most firmly in their minds.

This is not to say that Dan did not have a great sense of

humor. He loved a good joke, and he had many stories to tell his children. But even the stories, as almost every part of his whole being, were so totally committed to the goal of improving society through the work of humble peacemakers that much of what he did or said had a message of teaching the values implicit in that task. Though this was a rather prevalent idea of that time—an optimism that the world would get better and better if "we" worked hard enough—Dan's dedication and commitment to the idea bordered on the fanatical.

Though the farm was an arena of work, when Dan came home from a week or two-week trip he must have felt, "One is nearer God on a farm than anywhere else on earth." He put on old clothes, got something to eat from the refrigerator (something protein because he usually ate vegetable plates when traveling on church expense), and then went outdoors. First, a look at the wheat to see how it was progressing, or the corn, or maybe how the trees they had planted were growing. He came back in the house, still tired but somewhat refreshed, and made a comment something like this, "That's the finest wheat we've ever had." Usually it was a superlative statement about something growing on the farm. The children chided him a bit, as teenagers tend to do, about whether he was realistic—if the wheat was really better than it was last year or if the onions did taste better than they did two or three years ago. Later, however, they recognized that what their father was really doing was impressing himself again with the fact that things of nature were exciting and refreshing. They were alive and growing! This he liked.

Now it is popular to be conscious of the balance and conservation of nature. The West children learned early the principles of ecology. The policy, "Don't pick a flower until you can count ten of them for replenishment" was heeded by the children. Instructions for felling a tree were carefully followed by the boys so nearby trees would not be damaged. They learned to count the rings on the cross-section of a tree to discover its age. One of Dan's special arts, which he enjoyed very much, was making a mall, a wooden sledge hammer, to drive wedges to split the logs.

Dan's idea of conservation came up in another way. After

their move from Dunlap to a farm near Middlebury, Dan often took an early morning train out of Elkhart, through Chicago, and on into Elgin for a ten o'clock meeting. This necessitated someone taking him into Elkhart about sixteen miles from the farm. He allowed enough time, if everyone worked rapidly, to get up, get dressed, and start the car (assuming it would start right away) to drive the speed limit in Indiana (then about 50-60 on the highways, 25-35 in the city) so he could run through the station and board the train before it started to pick up much speed.

Dan was concerned about traveling fast. He recognized that it is not safe, and also that a car consumes more gasoline at a higher speed. Through the farmland on Route 20 out of Middlebury he suggested that the speed be kept "tolerable," meaning about 40. But as Elkhart city limits came into view, with about three miles of city driving left (two on a brick shortcut), Dan looked at his watch and realized that there were not as many minutes left as he had anticipated. So he suggested, "Step it up a bit." Step it up a bit might be repeated three or four times until 50 or 55 was reached in order to catch the train. This didn't seem to make sense to the children. Why not drive 50 or 60 in the country and then when in the city, slow down? And why couldn't their father get himself together enough to meet a train in decent time? It seemed to the children that they were always streaming into the station wide-eyed and breathless with their father's coattails flying as he boarded the already-moving train. Usually there was not time to bid his wife goodbye or wave farewell to the waiting family. But there was always a glow on his face; he seemed to be at his height of glory when going on a trip!

Perhaps these hurried and harried situations arose because there was the principle of conserving and driving safely, but there was also another principle—that of being efficient with one's time. Why get up a half hour earlier and have to stand waiting in the station? That's unacceptable too. What is interesting is that oftentimes Dan's general goals would conflict, and some compromise had to be made to reach the end result.

It was upon returning home from one of those wild, flying trips to Elkhart that the children heard their mother very slowly and deliberately pronounce the forbidden word, "Darn!" Everyone whooped it up and fell out of the car laughing and cheering, their mother included. It was a kind of celebration; their mother seemed very real, very human to them then.

It was Lucy who made the decision to sell the Dunlap farm and did the groundwork for the purchase of the larger farm near Middlebury. The children were older (Joel, 15; Jan, 13; the twins, Larry and Phil, 11; and Steve, 6). Lucy was beginning to feel her own strength by now. She had always been a very strong woman but played herself pretty low as all good women did at that time. The entire family was eager to move to Middlebury because the Mark Schrock family lived only four miles south. The Schrock children and other friends would be attending the same church and school.

On one cold wintry day in March, 1950, the move was made from the Dunlap farm to the 156-acre farm near Middlebury. Moving was a hilarious time with many trucks of friends there to help. Everything was moved and, with a lot of confusion, all of it finally got into the house. Everyone was very tired and very happy. The last ones to leave the Dunlap farm assured the others that Dan would soon be coming. It was an eleven mile trip and he would arrive later because he was driving Daisy and bringing the sleigh. It began to snow and time got later and later. Soon they heard him coming! He had put the sleigh bells on old Daisy. Bounding through the lane, snow falling, with sleigh bells ringing came Dan, smiling and happy with a kitten wrapped up in his coat. He had found her in the old house, now very cold, snuggled up against the few remaining live coals in the ash pit of the furnace. The children were impressed with Dan's unique way of climaxing the big move.

There were two houses on this new farm. After five years of renting the smaller house, the West family decided to help some refugee families resettle in America. One family came from Germany, another arrived from Amsterdam. This proved to be a broadening cultural and linguistic experience for the family. Later, when the refugees had established their own homes, a poor South Carolina family moved in; however, this one posed many problems.

In the fall, after the move to Middlebury, Lucy started teaching school again. She taught for eighteen years in the Middlebury schools and four in the Goshen system, most of the time with first-graders. They loved Lucy and delighted in her quiet, reassuring manner.

The work ethic became even more pronounced on the large farm. Dan was gone much of the time, but Lucy was a very capable woman who ably handled their day-to-day problems. She did not refer to Dan, saying, "When your father gets home . . . " or "I'll have to tell (or ask) your father . . . ." In a way life was less confusing when Dan was gone, for Lucy seemed a bit more relaxed. The decisions could be made quickly, and there was a singleness of thought on a subject. But they all looked forward to their father's return, and the work would fly so they would be free to do the fun things "when Dad got home."

Trips to the wooded area on the farm were always special. In the winter they went either to get a tree or to cut wood. In these early days of the crosscut saw, wedges, and bucksaws, there was a closeness as father and sons talked together while they worked. Later the chain saw made too much noise for really social times in the woods, but they continued to pack a lunch and get a plexy-full of wood for burning. (Plexy was an old, rundown manure spreader they hauled the wood in.)

One cold and clear day, with lots of snow on the ground, the entire family went out to cut wood. All day long they cut with the crosscut saw, building a fire in an old tree stump for lunch and heat. Loading the large wagon with wood and returning to their little hamlet of farm buildings in the evening just as the sun was setting created a beautiful and unforgettable scene. Around a crackling fire in the fireplace they sipped hot chocolate, the end of a memorable day.

For a fall junket the Wests took a trailer, about two picnics' worth of food, and drove to an old apple orchard where they picked up windfalls. The apples fell on chunks of baled hay, so they weren't badly bruised. With the trailer full and a few bushels of the best apples in the trunk of the car, they returned to Middlebury and dropped off the apples at the cider mill where they made cider and apple butter. The best were taken home—the Delicious for eating, the McIntosh for making and canning applesauce. Whenever similar jaunts were organized the whole family pitched in, having a "rollicking time," as Dan would say, returning tired but excited and full of laughter. Such excursions may have been fewer than for most families, but they seemed very special, maybe because they were fewer.

Most of the fun things centered around the farm rather than going to circuses and fairs. Dan would take the children swimming on occasion, but he did not delight in that kind of activity. He enjoyed people, talking to people, much more than just physical pleasures, such as lying in the sun or on the beach. He did enjoy hiking and invited the children and Lucy to join him on Sunday afternoons. Usually these treks were rather boring to the children as were the naps which were included in the Sunday schedule of many farm families.

Fun times together when Dan was home were great, but family decisions, seriously deliberated, proved to be "ho-hum, another one!" as the children got older. On Saturdays the family got up and had breakfast after the cows were milked and the rest of the chores were finished. The family council followed. One of the ongoing items was the dividing of the milk check. Although the amount each received was slim, the children were proud of the fact that the milking of the cows and the marketing of the milk was up to them.

Steve was not always convinced that it was fair. He often felt the authority of his older brothers who were given a good deal of control over him because of their father's absences. They had the power to recommend that his share of the milk check be docked. And docking did occur since Steve, five years younger than the twins, seemed to have a bit of difficulty getting up about 5:30 a.m. to help with the early morning chores.

When the children were young the list for the family council went something like this: what are the have-tos, the ought-tos and finally the want-tos? Together the family listed the tasks in that order, then worked them out as agreed. The most difficult to deal with was the ought-tos stuck in between the things you have to do and the things you want to do. Needless to say, the youngsters were resourceful enough to figure out how to put the want-tos right along with the have-tos so there was not really much suffering. It just seemed heavily structured.

No doubt Dan thought he carried out a policy of democracy in the council, but if anyone voiced an opinion contrary to his he usually said, "Do what you think is right" or "Which do you think would be best?" The children knew what their father thought, and when they were younger they complied with his wishes. As they grew older, however, they had had enough of the councils. At one family meeting the discussion centered around what crop to plant at the end of the property. After a lengthy consideration of the question, each member expressed his or her opinion. When it was his turn to speak, Joel, the oldest who had been away to college for a year, said, "Well, Dad, frankly I don't give a damn!" Just as years before when their mother said, "Darn!" the children laughed and celebrated.

Not too many family councils were held after that. To the children they seemed to be a kind of "exercise." This was disappointing to Dan, and though the children felt relieved, they felt a bit guilty for they had let their dad down. They were just too human; they couldn't live up to his expectations. But it was their way of establishing their own identity and asserting their own independence.

The procedure and idea of the family council was twofold. It was Dan's way of instilling in the minds of the children the importance of being concerned about the long-term consequences before the here-and-now kinds of concerns were considered. It was also his way of encouraging them to assume increasing responsibility for their actions in home and family decisions. Dan hoped their decisions would be in line with his. Sometimes they were, more often they were not. It was also Dan's attempt to become more involved and more influential in the family's activities and decisions. Because his vocational activities took so much time at home and away from home, he did not figure very prominently in the decision-making. Lucy had purchased the farm, and the fellows made the decisions about the animals, what crops to plant, when to cultivate and harvest.

Dan's idea of evaluating the long-term consequence when making decisions stuck with some of the children. It has allowed them to delay gratification on a large number of things, earthy and not so earthy. Joel is keenly impressed with the fact that that consideration is a result of his training. Joel cites a very simple example. When he was in college he decided he wanted a hi-fi system. He thought about it and looked in catalogs for the cost of a new one. Or, he could build a system himself, rent one, or get a used one from a local junk dealer. There were a variety of things he could do immediately, or he could wait a couple of years, and he did—seven or eight years. He recognizes that the attention to long-term consequences and long-term payoffs was deeply instilled in him and to some degree in his brothers and sisters as well.

9
Living
With a
Perfectionist

Dan West also believed in perfection. He worked hard to turn his beliefs into actions. Life was for doing things and accomplishing things—that in itself should be fun. His basic message, as seen by the children, was to strive to be perfect; and if you didn't succeed, just try harder and harder.

Phil, serving two years in Brethren Volunteer Service in Poland (1961-62) felt greatly relieved when he caught the meaning of grace at a Brethren conference which used as a text *The Cost of Discipleship* by Dietrich Bonhoeffer. He suddenly felt released from this tremendous burden of trying to be perfect, to be correct, to be right. It was good to be rid of that load; it felt good to be free, to be human, to relax and not strive so hard. Though angry with his father at that time for implanting the idea of perfection so firmly in his mind, he later saw his father as a representative of his time, a product of his time—as we all are—and in that historical sense, acceptance of his father was easier.

Grace did not seem to be a concept that Dan understood; or if he understood, he rejected it. And in the rejection of that part of Christian theology he was at the same time rejecting a kind of unconditional parental love and warmth to his children. What he imparted to them was conditioned upon their agreement, usually a silent commitment extracted from them, that they would take whatever he gave them and make it better. And that was exhausting; that was tiring. He always seemed to infer, "You did well, but you can do better." The task of doing right, doing what was good, was never-ending. They didn't feel they could rest the way they really were. Dan had an ideal of perfection which could never be attained.

Some of his children still feel a certain amount of guilt that they were never all their father expected of them; others no longer carry these feelings. Some have appreciated the pull to look at long-term consequences and long-term goals, while another asks, "Why did we need to go to such ends? What were we trying to prove? Just living didn't seem to be enough—just being ourselves, just being human. We had to be something more, something bigger. We couldn't be just plain United States citizens. We were citizens of the world."

While the drive instilled in them is now recognized, some still find it difficult to be relaxed, to live and enjoy the *now,* not always weighing what the future holds. The Wests were similar to many families whose goals are doing, achieving, and today, more than in Dan's time, accumulating. Perhaps the ideals were a bit higher for the West children because Dan had bigger goals.

While the West family lived on the farm near Middlebury, they became involved in a cooperative farm arrangement Dan had been advocating this idea throughout the church and it seemed logical that he should try to put his idea to work in the farm situation. Fifteen to twenty interested families in Northern Indiana had discussed cooperative proposals over a two to three year period, leading up to the Wests' move to Middlebury. For three years the Dan West and Mark Schrock families pooled their two farms and brought into the cooperative a third family, the male of which was to be in charge of the day-to-day activities on the two farms. This motivation was not primarily to make more money but to demonstrate that it would be possible to share tools and equipment in a communal farming arrangement. It was an experiment to see whether such a relationship was economically feasible. In this way, Dan and Mark thought, all the work could get done, all the boys (and there were plenty of them) could go to summer camp and still have time to go swimming in the swimming hole in the Little Elkhart River which ran behind the Pleasant Valley Church of the Brethren about four miles north of Middlebury.

It was basically an unstable situation with the farms four miles apart. After three years of experimenting, the arrangement folded. The only way the cooperative worked was in the economic arena; everyone made a profit, not so much in spendable cash for the coop members, but in cattle and other livestock. The equity that was built up in terms of equipment and land values was impressive.

With the plan for supervision ended, the West boys were left with no overseer. Because Dan could not fill the role of managing the farm, his wife had to assume much of the responsibility. To her, however, they were not years of drudgery. There was hard work to be done, but the family was always a team. They worked together and things got done! Lucy may have felt in times of fatigue, "This isn't quite fair," but she was able to bounce back with both emotional and physical energy. She said little, for Dan was doing what made him supremely happy. When he came home he brought fresh and exciting news, giving his family a worldwide vision of his dreams, the insights gleaned from his travels and new experiences, and the mind-stretching which always happened when he was home.

Lucy's biggest problem in those days was the concern and criticism of some outsiders, as well as the concern of her father and mother and some of her brothers and sisters, who felt sorry for her. They thought Dan worked too hard for the church and was gone from home too much. But they listened to, and gloried in, his sermons asking for total commitment and devotion to Christ and to a better world for everyone. Those were rough years spent in loving, accepting, and living with the uncommon man whose idealism worked well with a small group, over a short time, but which could not work as well with the more or less permanent, home-based group.

Dan depended upon the children and assumed that they would do their part when he was gone. From an early age Joel recalls his father, when leaving on a trip, telling him that he was counting on Joel to be the man of the house while he was away. There were some irritations, too. The younger boys remember Dan's habit of sending postal cards from Ft. Wayne or Cincinnati, just after he had taken off on one of his many trips. On the card he listed all the things he had forgotten to tell the family to do in his absence. This seemed hypocritical to the boys, as they realized he didn't have the time to devote the sort of energy they must exert to keep the farm going. But it indicated his desire to become more involved in the farm than he was functionally able to be.

Though perhaps resented at the time, many experiences on the farm gave the children skills, tools, resourcefulness, and pride which prepared them for active lives with a certain adaptability. The choice "to keep them down on the farm" was a wise one. One of the happiest days for the twins, however, was an early morning in April, 1956. As they were leaving for a train trip to New York and Washington, D. C. with their senior class, the milk cows were sold. They never milked their own cows after that. It was the end of one chapter of farm life for them.

Dan's idea of cooperative or communal sharing did not end with the experiment with the Schrocks. Neighbors up and down County Road 31 had manure spreaders and tools which were more modern than the old ones the Wests owned. Dan liked to have his family share tools, though they had less equipment than most of their neighbors. It cut costs, he said, but he also pointed out that the interdependence of neighbors helped to establish friendships and congenial relationships, a part of his idea of the "coming brotherhood." Maybe this was a good idea, but those still at home felt it was a bit unfair to foist this idea upon other families.

Yet some of the neighbors had less storage than the Wests who had ample barns, granaries, corncribs, and a shed on the premises. If the farmers up the road had a bumper crop or were in a hurry to harvest all their soybeans or corn instead of taking time to truck them to the elevator, Dan would offer the use of the granaries on his farm.

Sometimes he would buy the neighbor's product at the going price. This was, in a sense, speculating, but Dan seldom lost on a deal and usually made money. In this area, he was not quite willing to share; he was interested in making fifty cents a bushel. He reasoned that the granaries were being put to use and this was being frugal.

About the time each child was in fifth grade, Dan took that particular one on a major trip to the east or to the west coast. At the age of eleven Jan was offered this wonderful trip to California, a long two and one-half day train trip from Chicago. Not much was packed in her little suitcase, no new clothes bought, but the memory of thoroughly enjoying that trip with her father is still clear in her mind. He was very, very attentive, and that made her extremely happy. They talked with anybody and everybody about anything and everything. She reveled in the responsibility he gave her.

In Kansas City, where they were to spend the night with friends, Dan suggested that while he made a telephone call she should go into a restaurant, which he pointed out, and order her dinner. Apparently he had not looked over the place carefully. When he returned he found his daughter, sitting at the bar with a gentleman on either side, relating enthusiastically every detail of their trip west. Sternly, and seemingly out of character at the moment, he rushed her to a booth where proper little ladies of eleven should sit. This was her first caution that strangers, especially men, might not be trusted. (Likewise, one of the boys recalls being warned about the "women of the world." Dan's words served as a reminder that there should be a sound mixture of fear and trust in other people.)

While Dan attended to his business, he depended upon his daughter to take care of herself. Without any fear whatsoever she stayed with new friends, traveled alone from Los Angeles to Fresno on the train, and adapted herself well to many new situations. This made her feel very big, very proud of herself.

It was on these trips that the children saw their father at

his best. The personal attention and involvement with their father in his element—traveling endlessly and becoming involved with people and places, grappling with ideas and slowly nudging people to follow him in his plan—were the things that were exciting to them. This was his life, and he thoroughly enjoyed it. They sensed his happiness; it was his "food." The interaction with people, and their obvious pleasure at having him with them, filled him with elation. It was an eye-opener and very enjoyable from the point of view of the children since it involved so many people who already knew their father well and therefore received each of them very warmly too.

They recognized their father as being very, very happy, always on top of things, able to move quickly, to make decisions with dispatch. At home, when he was confronted with domestic situations—decisions on what to do with the fields, how to deal with farm life, how to relate to his family— they did not see him as being as happy nor as strong in making decisions.

On these trips they saw that his love for them took the form of enjoyment in seeing them observe what he enjoyed doing and knowing that their own horizons were being widened. But they missed expressions of warmth and physical contact with their father. He did not cuddle them, rarely hugged them or put his arm around them. Rather he would shake hands when he returned home from a trip. He didn't play hard, wrestle, or rough-and-tumble them, although he did seem to enjoy playing volley ball, the only physical way in which he seemed to work out his aggressions and frustrations. The tussling and romping of four children born within the span of six years (one set of twins) might have been quite rough and even threatening to their father. When they grew older and more boisterous in their relationships, they seemed to startle him. How could they be so full of energy and have this strong love/hate relationship with each other? This was something he had probably never experienced.

Although physically not demonstrative in his show of affection, Dan's smiles were sincere, and a certain joyfulness in his voice exuded warmth. He was conservative in his expression, disliking the gushy style of many. Thus, to the children, he always seemed rather guarded. Everything seemed to have a purpose; there was little spontaneity. Though he was so happy to have a family at last, he seemed awkward in expressing love, kindness, and joy in a physical way while still maintaining his image. Dan was probably no exception, for showing affection by physical expressions of touching was not generally the pattern in intra-family relationships in the 30s and 40s.

He would verbally express his affection but with little enthusiasm; he showed respect more than love and admiration. He was intellectually warm. In the exchange of ideas they felt love for him. Dan was an idea man, and after a Sunday dinner the seven of them would talk about philosophy and religion, and the world. He was able to get the children to expand their own consciousness and their own minds through his probing questions. Perhaps they also liked showing off to each other how skillfully they could use the language. Those were special times, and everyone enjoyed them.

Besides the intellectual discussions, the family enjoyed reading Shakespeare's plays. Dan had a friend in Middlebury, a puppeteer and a very talented theatre person, who delighted in the creative and responsive West children. He passed out the books of plays and everyone sat around and read Shakespeare aloud. They relished doing it and showing off! The neighbor complimented them whenever they read with animation or gave the reading a theatrical interpretation. Those evenings were wonderful. They all felt excited and exhilarated.

One of Dan's contemporaries who specialized in psychology rated Dan's native ability as superior. The quality of Dan's thought processes were uniquely individualistic. He was basically a qualitative thinker but his thinking set the pattern on which more practical and quantitative thinkers could build a strong and practical program, such as the Heifer Project. This native ability was apparent to his family also for he loved any intellectual game, task, or exercise. It was then that he seemed most animated because of his interacting.

One weekend in 1962, Joel, who was majoring in psychology, brought home the Wechsler Adult Intelligence Scale (WAIS) and gave the test to Dan. The test has many parts with each section starting off fairly easy and getting progressively more difficult. After you miss so many in a row, you no longer continue in that section, but go on to the next. Each part is timed, and Dan knew he was racing against the clock. It soon became apparent to him that he was winning, and he got very excited about it all. It seemed that he enjoyed testing his wings again and corroborating his impressions of his own skills. Needless to say, he scored extremely high— more than three standard deviations above the mean on that test—for his age group.

Dan enjoyed the cats and dogs on the farm, teasing and playing with them. But on a few occasions he did get angry at the animals. Prior to some transplanting in the spring Dan once lost his composure. The whole family had gone on an excursion to Goshen where some people, across from the Mill Race, had a greenhouse and raised plants for sale. Some very lovely plants, mostly vegetable plants, were purchased. Leaving those plants, carefully wrapped in damp newspapers on the porch, the seven Wests went inside to eat supper, pleased over the healthy specimens soon to be planted in the cool of the evening.

Dan was the first one out on the porch, eager to get started. There before him lay those fine plants strewn all over the porch, the yard, and the driveway. The dog, by pulling at the newspapers, had simply played havoc with the plants. Dan was irritated, angry. He did not forgive that dog very easily! That same mixed rat terrier had another run-in with Dan when he got into one of Dan's boots and put a few holes in it. Dan didn't get over that incident quickly either.

Some of the decisions made by fellow staff and board members angered Dan. Most of the time his anger was leveled at the idea, but sometimes he would speak indirectly about people in ways that suggested his anger might have been more personal.

Dan hated to get angry. He regretted any time he showed this part of himself, and at times it seemed that he was asking the family to take care of him or to protect him. For a couple of weeks they were asked to evaluate his actions during the week. Did he behave as a proper parent? Did he become angry? Did he show his temper in any way? Was he even-tempered? The latter was no doubt his goal. For the children this was tiresome and boring.

Health was one of Dan's personal concerns. He often told friends, "Yes, the conference went well; I went into it rested." Or on occasion, "The meeting was not so good; I was tired and didn't overcome it." Exercise was part of his health program. When traveling in a car with colleagues, he would run across the frontage of the service station several times while the attendant filled the car with gasoline. While playing run tag with the children—one of the few times he did so—Dan told one of the twins, then about ten years old, that already he could run faster than his father. Dan said he was not going to try to run because he couldn't. By the time the children were teenagers it became apparent that their dad did not have a lot of energy. He had considerable strength in his hands, he could walk well and had great endurance, but at a great expense to him physically. His modest energy level was reflected in the time it took him to do transplanting and small tasks in the garden. He enjoyed working there and the slow pace was a nice contrast to the schedule he kept. Perhaps it was his age, or his metabolic level, but Dan did not have a great deal of energy to draw upon.

To some degree he believed that foods made a difference in one's disposition and intelligence—"tell me what you eat and I'll tell you what you are"—so it was not surprising that Dan emphasized natural foods. Not only did he not drink coffee, tea, or soft drinks (he was too young, he'd say), but he preferred that his family not do so either. Lucy and Jan were visiting in the home of a friend one hot day. The host offered them a Coke. Jan looked appealingly to her mother, and Lucy nodded that it was all right, but the host suddenly realized that he had put them both on the spot.

At a Brethren Service Commission staff-family retreat, one staff member saw Dan's family for the first time and was surprised and a bit relieved to find them quite human and like everyone else. Lucy drank coffee because she liked it. She was her own person while living with all of Dan's disciplined life of not eating desserts, limiting the amounts of meat, and wanting milk at every meal. Lucy once asked a friend if she thought using cream was a sin, adding that Dan felt it was too extravagant and too much of a luxury for her to cook with it.

"I cannot eat cake when others do not have bread" brought mixed reactions from Dan's many hostesses and from his children. For some women, baking a pie or cake, or whipping up a lovely dessert was a way of making guests feel welcome and to show the family's happiness at their coming. To such persons Dan's rather curt and final statement seemed an affront to hospitality. Some felt his idealism at this point may have been correct but his reasoning a bit faulty. His sons and daughter knew he liked cake by the way he watched them eating their share. Did his not eating cake provide bread for others?

To other families who entertained Dan in their homes, his remark served as a reminder of their affluence, their full stomachs, while many people in the world were starving. It was one man's way of sacrificing for a cause. His words were recalled by many families as they guiltily finished off a big meal with a rich dessert. It is not surprising that of all of Dan's statements this one is probably the most remembered.

10
Prophet and Gadfly

Amid the bits and scraps of notes found among Dan's papers was a 3 × 5 card with the title "Christian Gamblers." It read: "The gambler's spirit, *not* his purpose or tools or methods is akin to 'nerve' or 'faith' as I learn a bit more of the meaning of the Bible and God's working in the world. Ahead of time nobody can predict the outcome of discussions on race relations or world peace or the home or anything else we know; including this obstreperous youngster of this class of juniors. In trust of God's power we take a chance when the odds are against us. This is a bit like the scripture, 'While we were yet sinners, Christ *died* for us.' That is the biggest gamble I ever heard of." Then he quoted M. Slattery on the same card: "This world would be a better place were it not for the timid friends of God."

No one can say Dan was a "timid friend of God." He was determined about rightness and wrongness—very positive, almost to the point of being dogmatic. Dan could be rigid and uncompromising at times when integrity and values were being compromised. Yet he was also adept at conceding on insignificant points and adaptive to a degree, as long as his long-range values were not dissipated.

Among laypersons and leaders whose life patterns were well established and who did not wish to open these patterns for re-examination, Dan was apt to be an unwanted irritant, particularly if he raised questions about their life-style or some value or belief which those individuals held dear.

For those who worked closely with Dan there were times when the going was difficult. He had original ideas, strong convictions, and was creative and persuasive in trying to get his ideas accepted and promoted. But when things did not go to his liking, he was often given to silence. A fellow worker, returning home from a staff meeting, seemed noticeably discouraged and down-hearted. His wife, sensing his mood, asked the reason. Her husband responded, "Oh, it was one of Dan's silent days! I guess that is his privilege."

As a staff person employed by a national church board, Dan often frustrated his co-workers. He was not a team man. He wanted to call his own shots. He was annoyed at any kind of supervision. He wanted to live where he chose and do as he wanted with his time. He was the kind of employee who makes difficulties for administrators. His request to move his office from Elgin, the staff headquarters, to his home on a farm near Goshen, Indiana, with secretarial help to be provided there, was contrary to the best ideas of administration, but because the Board did not want to sever the relationship or lose his help, his request was granted.

His colleagues in the Elgin offices were not always happy with Dan. Fellow workers chafed at his refusal to live in Elgin as part of what he called "identifying with the grass roots." He wanted to know what people in the local churches were thinking, the questions they were asking, and ways Elgin staff members could best serve them. There were those who felt that this was definitely a privilege; they, too, would have enjoyed such an opportunity. Why shouldn't he live in Elgin as part of the staff rather than coming just for meetings which were sometimes called at his convenience?

Not only did Dan not cooperate well with the organization; he often bucked it. He disliked "big things" and "respectability" and that meant the "upper" church administration and the administrators who wore business suits to look respectable. He grew restless with any kind of routine, disliked being told what he could do, and was irritated at having to "go through channels." The latter attitude was particularly evident

at the 1948 Annual Conference when the youth were propos-
ing to get the Brethren Volunteer Service program before the
conference as an impromptu issue, rather than going through
the regular procedure for agenda items. Dan inferred, if he did
not actually say, "Who says we can't do it?" and took it on as
challenge to prove that it could be done.

Pursuing his own pet projects, he often seemed to ignore
other aspects of the church's life and work. His visits to
churches to talk with young people about peace and volunteer
service without consulting the pastors in advance caused some
criticism in his early leadership days. Parents became alarmed
at some of the revolutionary ideas he advocated for their youth.
Both groups often felt he was dividing the church by his
radical views. Some college presidents were irritated when he
appeared on campus unannounced.

At one time a kind of feud seemed to exist between Dan
and college presidents. Asked why he didn't appear at one of
the educational institutions more frequently, Dan simply
replied, "I don't have time to go everywhere I am invited and
to those places where I am not invited." Persons in ad-
ministrative positions felt he belittled them when he quoted,
"Bishops are not evil people; bishops are feeble people," a
phrase he had heard a vicar make in a high-church worship
service in Thaxted, England. Dan seemed to delight in telling
the story of a layman who was determined to introduce a
bishop "just right." He planned ahead to use the phrase,
"revered and venerated," but got mixed up in the actual introduction and it came out instead, "veneered and renovated."

Dan challenged church bureaucrats to be more sacrificial
in service and leadership. Often he acted as a conscience to denominational boards and their administration. He did not ad-
just easily to organizations and since he was not the ad-
ministrative type, he seemed unable to see their point of view.
Dan was a "why" man, not a "how" man. His approach was
different in many respects. He contended that if the *right people* want something, they can get speedy action. *Persons,*
rather than institutions, were important in getting a program
carried out. Dan was a philosophical leader, an idealist, a policy
former. He was not about to become a cog in the machine of

administration. Dan was his own man with his own particular philosophy. Yet he was deeply committed to the church generally, and to the Church of the Brethren, though he was restless and impatient with its ways. Dan never forsook his church; he loved it and worked diligently for its basic beliefs.

While he may have been a problem to administrators, to youth Dan was a breath of fresh air! Many young persons had become disenchanted with the church. Young college graduates had worked hard in youth and children's work and were troubled to find that the way of Christian love taught to the children in the basement was not practiced in the council meetings upstairs. Struggles between differing elements in a church produced hurtful results in the life of a congregation. These youth often felt torn apart by the situation because they loved and respected people on both sides of the controversy.

A young woman, sitting in the balcony one Sunday morning, looked down over the congregation thinking about the stormy council meeting of the past week and the gossiping on the telephone following the council. "If this is the religion of Jesus Christ, it isn't much!" she thought. "The *life* of the congregation is destroying what we are trying to teach." She felt embarrassed by the church's trouble and unable to cope with it. At times she felt like ditching the whole agonizing thing. Then along came Dan!

A young man in his 20s frequently found churches dull and unchallenging. The church, he felt, seemed hardly aware of the powerful forces he saw shaping society at that time. He was critical of the unreadiness or inability of many churches to become a more adequate and more Christian society in miniature. Gossip and immature behavior caused congregations to be torn apart, or to limp along with no thought of improving their conditions or relationships. He sighed resignedly, "If this is what the Christian faith is all about, I want no part in it." Then along came Dan! His concepts, questions, and approaches were like a cool, refreshing, and stimulating breeze. The dull became tolerable; the problems became challenges.

These expressions could speak for the feelings of hundreds of youth in the 30s and 40s. Dan listened. He challenged. He sought out the loner. He saw tremendous potential in youth and they felt his confidence. He was hopeful and believed that persons could change and were changing. He had every reason to believe that, for he saw many "ugly ducklings turn into swans," to use one of his favorite phrases. He believed that changed persons could change the world. He identified with youth, recalling major changes in his own life, frequently speaking of how green he had been as a youth.

Where did he lead them? To become caravaners and speak out for peace in the world. To become "Dunkers for Peace." To serve in work camps. To volunteer for church service for two years. To reject military service and choose Civilian Public Service. To teach in Africa through alternative service. To believe in the church in spite of its imperfections. To live like the Master!

Some of Dan's followers saw Dan not only as a prophet but also as an educator, a better prophet because he was an educator. Others felt that he had no educational system and they were puzzled because they saw education as mostly content. Dan was convinced that process, the right process, or an adequate process, was vital to learning. Learning that made a difference frequently required admission of prejudice, or blind spots, then further on a change of heart or attitude. Education, he believed, was not simply a matter of factual information. Dan insulted some college authorities because he thought of varied experiences, other than those in the classroom, as providing students with opportunities which were the equivalent of, or more valuable than, college learning. If persons did not know that Dan believed in learning through doing, if they had a low regard for process as a part of learning, then Dan made no sense and might offend.

Sometimes he was not diplomatic about it all. Why? Partly because he was reluctant to start back at the beginning and explain his beliefs in the preciousness of the process before he got on with the other points.

Dan spoke more often of approaches than of systems. He believed that experimentation and study through the results of workshops necessitated a review and evaluation of process.

Dan always encouraged individuals to learn by doing. He wanted them to help build the agenda, to contribute their own ideas, and to do some "big muscle" work, as well as to experiment in carrying out the plans.

Dan was a dreamer. He dreamed of a society as it should be; he saw persons as they could become. One minister in 1955 wrote: "I regret there are so few dreamers left in the world, for I sincerely believe that these are the men who the world so terribly needs today: men of vision who might for a moment soar beyond the realities of the present and grasp a sudden insight into a greater meaning in life, see a greater purpose for humanity, give it some hope, some inspiration which might in the future lift it out of its stifling, mechanistic muck of materialism." Dan was this kind of dreamer.

Many people have had a profound respect for Dan. Some have agreed with his ideas but disagreed with the means he used. Others have disagreed with his ideas but have regarded him as one of the great prophets of his time. Prophets do not fit into conventional molds. Prophets often have to present ideas that are radical and even excessive in order to be heard. Nor can we expect prophets always to be consistent or easy to live with. Prophets are visionary; they live in and out of the everyday world.

Dan West believed that Christians are called to be the gadflies who puncture the false popular concepts in social and economic systems. When everybody seems to be going in the same direction, it is time to question, perhaps even to turn around and go the opposite way. While Dan usually applied this to militarism, he was a perennial gadfly, always prodding persons into serious thinking in a multitude of areas. And Dan had ideas on almost every subject.

In a letter to a colleague he tackled the question of church architecture: "(1) The special values which should be suggested in a Dunker church are: stability and openness, simplicity, small groups, space for larger groups. But also equality that belongs to brotherhood. I see no special reason to glorify any special speaker." (Dan seldom spoke from a pulpit or any raised area, believing that all persons were on the same level.) "(2) What should be left out: likely pulpits, choir lofts, split chancels, crosses. I saw too many of them in Spain and just recently I read that to the Jews the cross symbolizes oppression.

"Also we would deliberately omit all costly items which keep us up with the Joneses. The Church of the Savior has no organ. No feeling that it is wicked—just is not needed and money could be better spent elsewhere.

"(3) What have we been underplaying? The love feast and sometimes baptism. Neither of these are 'musts' as I see them but they belong to the dramatization of adult believers and persons needing forgiveness and reconciliation often. Also we have been underplaying the active involvement of the large portion of worshipers and thinkers and planners, except to repeat words someone else thought up to say. . . . "

The relocation of the Bethany Theological Seminary from the Garfield Park area of Chicago to its present site in the suburbs was a matter of concern for Dan. He, as many others, had questions about the flight from the city. He felt there was a need for Brethren to try to help with the multitude of problems which existed there. The relocation in such an affluent community as Oak Brook also bothered Dan. At the same time he recognized that it was difficult for the Seminary to recruit students with families when crime was rampant in the community. If the decision could be based on the premise of being morally right versus a decision as to what most of the constituency wanted to do, Dan would be inclined to say, "Let us decide to do what we ought to be doing and then get on with it." Though Dan was a visionary, he was practical enough to see that the ideal is not always possible.

Dan did not have a favorable view of the Boy Scouts. He thought there was something militaristic about the movement and pointed to their motto: "Be Prepared." A Boy Scout leader, in discussion with Dan, pointed out quickly the correct meaning and use of the motto—to be prepared for emergencies, to be prepared for undertakings of any kind, to be prepared for life. Dan didn't argue any further, but he continued to believe that the formalizing of patriotic exercises—saluting the flag and pledge of allegiance—and the uniforms were somehow militaristic. His views on peace were not simplistic; he recognized the complexities, but he stood uncompromisingly against even a suggestion of anything militaristic.

During the 30s and 40s many missionaries felt that Dan was critical of their effort and movement, though he had never visited a foreign mission field until he retired. He was enthusiastic about practical aid—food, clothing and shelter—for the needy, refugees, war-torn sufferers, and the destitute, the "little people" of the world. He did not seem to realize then that the same kind of practical aid was also a primary concern to the missionaries. It seemed that Dan never got completely away from his original concept of missionary work in terms of preaching and converting sinners. He believed strongly in the convictions of early leaders of the Church of the Brethren, who urged, "No force in religion." Dan applied this to economic, social, and political pressures, as well as to the old types of overt compulsions applied in the days of his childhood. To share the Brethren understanding of religion with others, basic as that may be, was not enough. People hunger first for bread; second, for truth, Dan believed.

Later in his life when he visited in India, he changed his ideas regarding missionary efforts. He was impressed with their accomplishments. Seeing was believing.

Dan wanted church people to have a "latch-string out" policy so that travelers in any area would feel free to stop and spend the night with fellow Christians. This, he said, would strengthen the fellowship and develop a closer community feeling among the members of the faith. Dan practiced what he preached. He was known to drop in for a meal or to spend the night with or without any prior arrangement. Few complained because Dan's stimulating conversation and his broad knowledge of world affairs made him a pleasant and welcomed guest.

The same attitude prevailed when he traveled with others. At one Annual Conference Dan asked to ride home with a neighbor-pastor. The time for leaving had been agreed; all the others arrived and waited and waited. For over an hour they waited. Upon his arrival Dan jumped in the car without an apology. Along the way he remembered that a friend lived not far off the road. Would they stop for a minute? Again, they waited while he visited with his friend. Dan valued every one of *his* minutes, even disliking to wait a few minutes for a train or plane. To Dan such common courtesies of travel, good or bad, were assumed to be part of being Brethren.

In the late 20s, Dan was advocating the limiting of one's income—consciously, intentionally, consistently, and conscientiously. He felt that everyone should "peg his income." This concept was a hard one to think through or to accept and few could live with it or by it. One colleague suggested that this was probably the watershed idea that alienated certain of his (Dan's) Southern Ohio enthusiasts.

Dan also proposed that expense accounts for church committees should not be the same for all members. Actual need, he contended, should be the basis for determining payments. One Elgin co-worker pondering the mechanics of such a process sighed, "Complicated! *Who* would decide the need?"

In terms of salary Dan did peg his income by refusing to accept a raise while serving on the national staff. But economically the farm was financially worthwhile for the family, almost embarrassingly so for Dan. It was the farm along with his wife's checks for teaching in the public school, not the checks which Dan got from the General Brotherhood Board, that sustained the family.

Putting "a voluntary ceiling on your wants" was a corollary which followed quite naturally. Dan challenged women to find clothing that suited them and their life-style. He urged them not to change with every whim of the fashion world.

One teacher had bought an inexpensive fur coat and a Pontiac car during her first year of teaching. Later, through Dan's influence, she went into a volunteer service program. Her unit spent a week in Plymouth, Indiana, where they took a survey of a slum section of the town. Though it was a very cold winter, she opted to wear a thin jacket rather than to offend those people by wearing her fur coat. She had decided the fur coat said something about herself which she did not want to convey, and so she got rid of it; it was not consistent with her new emerging life-style. Soon a Volkswagen took the place of the Pontiac.

Dan's own appearance was once described by Leland

Wilson, a Brethren pastor: "He wears a cream-colored sport shirt, open at the collar, and a pair of wash trousers. Long before the dress revolution, when education and nonlaboring men were expected to wear business suits, he chose to ignore that convention. Whether by design or by self-expression, the very clothing that covered his back identified him with the people of the common way, not with the people of power."

In going through Dan's files and notes I found jottings written on the back of used envelopes, on scraps of paper, on 3 × 5 cards—on almost anything he might have had handy when on a train, in a car, researching in a library, or musing at work. On the back of one yellowed and fragile envelope were these relevant quotations:

"That man is richest whose pleasures are the cheapest."

"To be content with little is difficult, to be content with much is impossible."

"A man is rich in proportion to the number of things he can afford to let alone.—H. D. Thoreau"

"Economy is an important virtue and debt can be a danger to be feared."

"If you give money, give yourself with it.—H. D. Thoreau"

"Spend less than you get."

And then this timely and penetrating question: "Do you spend more than you make on things you don't need to impress people you don't like?"

Quite an accumulation of quotations on one small, used envelope!

11
The View From Spain

In 1936 the many leftist parties in Spain united in a "Popular Front" to overwhelm the conservatives and moderate liberals in the national vote. Civil war followed within a few weeks. The rebels, who called themselves Nationalists, were the conservatives, led by General Francisco Franco and the Spanish Army. The defenders were the government and its workers, called the Loyalists. Both sides committed atrocities in bitter fighting. For the first time large-scale aerial bombing of civilians was carried out, including a raid in 1937 that destroyed the Basque town of Guernica. By the end of the war in March 1939, Spain had been devastated. A million Spaniards had been killed. Many were imprisoned by the new regime and more than 300,000 political refugees left Spain for exile in Mexico, France, or the U.S.

The conflict has been called a "training ground for the second World War," because other nations took part and tried new military tactics.

A committee on Spain was organized by the Brethren, the Friends (who took the initiative), and the Mennonites —the three historic peace churches in the United States.

It was anticipated that the church would not only provide financial support for the project but also send personnel in supervisory and service positions. M. R. Zigler, executive secretary, secured the approval of the Board of Christian Education of the Church of the Brethren for

Dan to go as a salaried worker to spend five months (Sept. 1, 1937 to January 1, 1938) in directing the relief program in the war-torn country of Spain.

Zigler was eager for Dan to accept the task because he wanted Dan to be the one to develop Brethren policy. When Dan's wife, with two small children at home, asked "Why Dan?" M. R. replied, "Dan has a world vision; a better concept than any one else I know."

In the magazine of the Hundred Dunkers for Peace, *Brethren Action,* June 1, 1937, Dan listed four reasons for wanting to go to Spain: (1) If Europe breaks into war, cooperation in Spain will be the springboard for neutral work for any later way; (2) my work there will be to save lives—especially mothers' and children's; (3) there is no direct way to stop the Spanish War; this is the best indirect way to help out; and (4) it may help to let everybody know that we are working on both sides."

While Dan was helping to plan the program of cooperation for relief work in Spain, M. R. Zigler had a different problem at home. As one observer put it, "Dunkers are slow to act, but give them time and they will help to a man if they are convinced." Convincing was M. R.'s task. The support for the program had to come from the people in the local churches. M. R. had learned through years of experience that "some of us have to watch our steps to see that we do not get too far ahead." Though Dan could dream dreams, it took a person like M. R. to see how those dreams could be fit into the total church program. Their approach to the peace problem was different but in looking back M. R. said, "Dan and I needed each other in our assigned tasks. I see that more clearly now than I did then.

M. R. did his job well and reported to the Annual Conference of June 1937 that "everyone seems to be enthusiastic about our Spanish Relief Program."

Sailing from New York on the S. S. Georgic on September 4, 1937, Dan was eagerly looking forward to his assignment. The following excerpts from Dan's letters to his wife, Lucy, were later printed in *Brethren Action.* While on the ocean he did a bit of introspection. "It's funny, I don't react to people here as I do on land. I can't explain it fully, rather guess it's partly the heavy job ahead, partly the fact that most of the people are not the simple, humble people I prefer."

London was the first stop in Europe where he conferred with some officials. "We were invited to worship with the Quakers," Dan wrote. "After some silence a Mr. Davidson read these words from his notebook: 'Whatever I have been able to achieve—in personal poise, stability, adequacy—has come to me by way of obstacles I have met. This has always been true of man since dawn. Darkness produced the lamp, fog the compass, winter clothed us, hunger drove us to exploration. The aviator must face the wind if he is to rise. This is a truth powerful enough to sustain me until I die. I know that in spite of all painful circumstances I have met, my course is upward. The universe is on my side; it will not let me down.'" Is it any wonder these words struck a responsive chord with Dan!

From London Dan went to Paris where he obtained his papers from the Prefecture of Police which enabled him to get from France to Spain—as far as the French were concerned. His word picture of rural France is delightful: "Stone and brick walls to shelter gardens—slender poplars with quaking leaves, some with bunches of mistletoe—fields like patch work quilts—sturdy houses and churches with low red-tiled or thatched roofs—lazy fisherman in boats and on shore—young couples out for a Sunday afternoon stroll—long pumpkin fields with big bold ovals rising above the leaves—neat roads wet and glistening in the sunshine after the shower—clean greying wheat stubble—it's beautiful. . . . "

Then a striking figure of speech: "In Paris I got two letters from you, but I know there are more on the way. It is a bit like looking at the stars. It takes long for the light to arrive when it has been coming all the time."

On to Burgos, Spain where fighting had taken place about eight months before, leaving a number of houses in complete ruin. "The children began to gather as the word was sent around, and within fifteen minutes perhaps twenty had come. They needed clothes, and were shy and dirty, but curious and eager to see and to get something. By the time we were through more than thirty children and nine mothers had come and all had received something. . . . You should have seen them crowd around for woolen stockings. Then the children and the mothers went back home, glad because somebody cared enough. I am glad our church took hold of this project. We need to be grappling more with world problems, and to offer our best help toward their solution. That means we must learn much more, and put our doctrine into action. Only so will we fulfill our mision."

October 10 in Burgos: "Today we ordered from London $75 worth of stockings, $225 worth of shoes, and $300 worth of underwear, all for children from two to twelve years old. Also we ordered $100 worth of Cocoa and milk powder. Tomorrow we want to order $200 worth of cod liver oil. These three items plus milk will be our specialties on food, but we want to emphasize clothing more up to January because of the cold weather."

October 17 in Bilbao: "I awoke this morning with the help of a rooster and church bells. It was pleasant outside, and I though of sunrise. Dressing hurriedly I went down to the street, out across the river, and climbed the hill on the other side. The sky was clear and I could see the rosy mist between me and the mountains to the southeast. While I had turned my gaze away for a bit the sun peeped out from behind the mountain—and there was morning. I got the general lay of the town and so felt more at home when I returned. It lies in a hollow of both sides of a winding river. The red tile roofs, very flat and close together, are in beautiful contrast with the green, steep hillsides."

The next day the group received their "general salvo conductor" (safe conduct papers) so they were free to go anywhere in Nationalist Spain except the war zone. After one month in Spain, Dan reported that he wished they could have done more, but additional goods were beginning to arrive, his Spanish was better, and soon they would be visiting eleven needy villages in Viscaya province—four of them in the mountains where winter would come early. If clothing from America didn't arrive soon, Dan feared the people would suffer greatly.

October 24: "This morning I hiked up a steep hill to the east to attend church at the Iglesia de Begona. The building is a magnificent stone basilisk looking down from the older village on the city of Bilbao. Through several opened round windows between the buttresses over the middle roof, the sunlight streamed. The windows lower down shone with a glory of color of their own. There were small holes in some of them and the shafts of light down through the incense-laden air were beautiful.

"I have to marvel at the simple faith of the worshipers. Many carried their kneeling chairs around as they stopped to kneel before the figure of now one saint, now another. All women wear the black mantilla, a thin veil; I think the same scripture is the source for that as for our prayer veil.

"This afternoon I finished reading the New Testament through—I think it was my first time. I did some thinking too:

"Jesus was a much more aggressive Person than I was taught in my youth, and intelligent beyond our present knowledge.

"John softened with years; he doesn't sound like a son of thunder when he writes about loving one another.

"Peter lost his impetuousness, but gained in power with years.

"Paul had a constant internal struggle; pride and humility, law and love, a constant self-consciousness; and he had a fixation on Jesus which reminds me of a girl writing to a friend about her lover. That makes him more understandable.

"I used to think I grew up in poverty, and the neighbors thought so too. But I've changed my mind. This, too, is relative, but there are many more millions in the world below that level than there are above it. I am convinced that we must do much because of the rare chance we have had. 'To whom much has been given. . . . '"

November 7: "I still marvel at the simple faith of these people—going to mass regularly, bending the knee when they enter and when they leave and whenever they happen to cross the middle line of the church. Sometimes the soldiers stoop so low in bending the knee that their bayonets in the sheaths at their sides almost touch the floor."

Word came to Dan that Earl Smith, a fellow relief worker, had failed to raise his arm during a celebration at which he was a guest—he did not know it was expected—and so he was fined rather heavily and confined to his apartment.

Dan went to see him on November 9. While on the train he made a list of lovely things: "The giving of breakfast at the Red Cross; tinted clouds in the east; a girl rubbing her dog's ear as he leaned against her knee at the station . . . oxen with sheep skins over their heads pulling a modern plow . . . young poplars with upreaching fingers, old poplars with tufts of branches along the trunk; the 'gracias' of a pale young woman after an hour standing when a soldier gave her his seat . . . the plaintive melody of a soldier's song; yellow chrysanthemums in front of a cloister . . . clean little gardens still trying; white sheets and other linen drying on the grassy slope by a creek; a triple-arched Roman bridge, partly ivy-covered, over a small stream away out in the country . . . red geraniums blooming by the doorstep of a white-walled cottage; twelve youngsters playing teeter on a pile of railroad ties."

Since November 7, when the goods arrived in port, the Red Cross had been unable to get them off the ship for distribution. Finally, on November 12, Dan met a man who offered to help him get information and action. "The way he barged in over red tape would have delighted an American gogetter. He carried the ball for some long gains and needed no interference. For a week I had waited for an answer to my letter to the Governor here. He took my carbon copy and got an answer in half an hour. He thinks it a shame that I have had to wait when the goods are here and cold weather is beginning. I could not help agreeing with him."

Earl Smith was released and arrived to join Dan. Together they visited an orphanage for children in a tiny valley east of Bilbao. Here a senorita who evidently had wealth in the past had spent it all taking care of the underprivileged orphans of all nations so that she had hardly enough to live on herself. Evidently she did not care as she found great meaning in life through helping the needy children.

"About sixty boys, a few not as large as Joel [Dan's and Lucy's oldest son, not quite 3½ years old], but likely older, take their exercises while singing the multiplication tables and the rules of Spanish grammar.

"The girls are learning embroidery work. They work colored designs on cotton by counting the threads. It is as fine as anything I have seen from China or India and must be fearfully hard on the eyes. In another room they made stockings to organ music. I am in favor of that. In a third room somebody makes shoes when they can get the leather. We may buy some supplies for them from England, instead of buying shoes which some need so badly."

November 15: "I am very happy tonight. After all these weeks of waiting we got the first part of our goods which we ordered in September, and I gave out 45 blankets to the Asylum of Merciful Love. I think I can sleep a little better tonight because I know 45 more children will be warmer as the result of a long process of which I am a part."

November 19: "At Ortuella, fifteen or more mothers came to see and get for their needy ones. . . . Smith insisted that none get two pairs of shoes until everyone had had a chance at one pair. One mother seemed almost greedy, but I cannot blame her. She did get two pairs of little shoes at that. The underwear was the most popular. We gave the boxes and string to the children and they were tickled. At Gallarta more than one-third of the three hundred children who eat regularly at the comedor (dining room) were there waiting when we arrived. About seventy were allowed to come into the hall and told to sit on chairs. They obeyed quickly. The girls who help there were ready to assist us in getting the shoes tried on the poorly clad feet and in distributing the underwear . . . . At Figueras a group of children sang the national anthem for us. It closes with a shout 'Arriba España.' (Arriba means up, high, aloft) That touched us. Because we had helped them just a little they felt warm toward our country. I wish we could build goodwill with the children all over the world. Then we could have peace on earth."

December 1: The comedor at Oviedo had been bombed during the fighting and a shell had killed some of the children just as they went out after a meal. "It was hard to see the youngsters walk past the blankets which they could not have. I was hoping that those who were selected to receive them could wait until the others had gone, but I guess it could not happen.

One boy of four or five was chosen to receive a blanket, and I wondered if he could get it home. I folded it up for him and he walked off into the night. But I rather guess someone took it from him as soon as he got out the door, as there was a commotion there. I don't blame the taker—just sorry for the little boy."

As the relief workers traveled throughout the countryside, they saw once-beautiful little villages which had been bombed until not one house was standing. When they came to the town of Ubidea, they asked that only thirty of the neediest should come to the plaza (public square), but 75 came instead. "The hard part was having to refuse some of the needy who came in hope and had to go home empty-handed. It was very rough on me, but we had come to help the neediest only—not everybody. A few children poorly clad with sores on their faces would have touched you deeply."

December 16, at Azpeitia, home of St. Ignatius Loyola founder of the Jesuit order, 1534: "While we have to wait for our goods to get out of customs, I suggested coming over here to visit the birthplace of Loyola and to learn all we can about him. I just finished a letter to Schwalm [his college history professor] who helped me to get interested in the man, along with Luther and Erasmus, nearly twenty-one years ago. History has been alive since for me, but now I care more and more to help make it. Loyola's ideas of absolute poverty, absolute chastity, and absolute obedience I cannot accept, altho (sic) I must respect what happened as the result of blocking the big urges of life for the purposes of his movement."

The marble, the copper, the gold chests and altar built by gifts from all over the world bothered Dan. "I wonder what he (Loyola) would say if he were to come back—he lived in poverty," wrote Dan.

"The simple faith of these worshipers always touches me, but I have some long, long thoughts. I wonder what the worship of the Virgin does to them. The lights, the incense, the robes, the crossing, the ornate fixtures, the sober faces, the images, the pictures of important religious events and of battleships, the tablets and statues—they certainly do something."

Christmas away from home was celebrated by a Christmas Eve dinner at the home of a Spanish friend. At midnight they attended the Misa del Gallo (Mass of the Rooster). Pageantry and communion lasted until 1:30 a.m. Musing with the other relief workers as to the special meaning of Christmas, Dan began, "To me Christmas is a promise, not fulfilled yet after more than nineteen centuries; it could have happened 1,000 years ago if those who called themselves Christian had risked all they had for it; it will happen some day, and we can help to hasten the process if we will; it includes an intensification of home life, and the growth of the spiritual organism which will make world peace possible."

Leaving Bilbao on December 31 (Dan's birthday), was hard for Dan had learned to like the Basque people very much. "But now that I am out of the country I will say 'Thank God' for a chance at free air again (relatively free, of course). I have had an opportuniy for another important part of my education and I am grateful. But it makes me more grateful for the rare chance we have in the USA.

I'm tickled that I got to help Smith pack a big box of socks, shoes, and underwear for needy children today before I left. Nineteen years ago today I used a six pound sledge hammer on defective aluminum mess kits in the army, flattening them out so nobody could use them and so they would take less space. I prefer this way of celebrating birthdays."

Returning to France to go through the Paris Embassy so he could get into Loyalist Spain, Dan arrived in Valencia on January 11, 1938. He wrote, "I have had a heavy meal of suffering—enough for me for one day. In the Seminary, where formerly Catholic priests were trained, live 2500 refugees, sometimes six in a moderate-sized room and one hundred in a long large room. For three or four months this Seminary has been used for refugees and considering everything it is fairly clean—my nose wasn't seriously offended.

"The building, with several stories and three inner courts, is very beautiful. The money and labor and perhaps hope put into this visible form might be justified if the priests who came through their training here had really been helpful to the problems of the people. It is four centuries since Loyola, and more than ten since Christianity had a strong foot-hold here. That is long enough. A church with a chance like that can be indicted for not doing its duty. And I can understand the fury of those who want to be rid of it.

"The only place incense arises now is in the kitchen, and that is the steam from the hot soup. The soup (chick peas and rice) looks good, but it would not make a satisfactory meal. Two hundred pounds of rice go into soup for 2500 people. That is 2½ ounces of the mixed foods per person, and each one gets about 50 grams (two ordinary slices) of bread. That is all for their noon meal, and only the 280 children get anything in the morning. For supper they have beans and another chunk of bread. There is no water or soap for washing in the Seminary.

"As we were leaving the upstairs open corridor—lovely stone pillars and rounded arches—I noticed a pile of bones lying near the wall. It looked as though someone had had several chickens. I asked our guide about it. He said no, they were the bones of a cat. And they were picked clean. When any of the folks can catch a cat they have a bit more to eat."

January 18, at Barcelona: This letter was started in the police station where Dan was under arrest—for four hours. Dan wanted to get to Barcelona on the only train leaving from Valencia. Because of preparations for another heavy offensive in the North, the seats were all sold and it was against the law to sell standing room. Finally, after much haggling, Dan got his ticket to stand and boarded the train. When the train stopped at a station, Dan wrote in his diary. Soon he noticed that one of the trainmen became suspicious of him. He asked for Dan's passport, then to see Dan's notes. Dan showed him the book cheerfully though it did little good for he couldn't read English. Upon arrival at the railroad station at Barcelona, Dan was taken to the police station to see if his notes contained anything "contrary to the cause." Though it was not to take long, Dan sat and sat. Asking several times if he could call friends in the city, he was finally given permission to call. The friend then notified the American consul. The Vice Consul arrived, translated the notes, and Dan was released.

January 19: When Dan's friends took him to the airport to leave Spain, they heard the chatter of an airplane and saw people running to refuge. They stopped the car (required by law) and got into a street car for a safer roof. Looking up they saw three silver colored planes, two miles high, flying to the southwest in almost perfect formation. The planes were leaving after dropping bombs near the railroad station a half mile away. A smoke cloud was rising from the fire that was started. "I can't say I was afraid," wrote Dan, "But I was concerned— and curious. Some risk? Yes, but when you want to help children you don't think so much about it, and it gives a lift to one's living. Terminado!"

(Over the Mediterranean) "Being suspended between the waters above the earth and those on the earth is interesting. We are trusting to mechanical applicances and to the skill of the pilots that we shall arrive safely. It gives a sense of reality to 'faith'. . . . "

Dan's stories of his experiences in Spain were graphic. In a talk at the West Goshen (Indiana) Church of the Brethren one Sunday evening, he told about a Spanish woman boiling bones two, three, and four times. "You'd be surprised how much good you can boil out of some old bones," he quoted her as saying. That story was not forgotten. It gave hunger a human face, and the persons hearing the story felt it through Dan's sensitive face.

Stopping by to visit Dan and Lucy the day after Dan's return home from Spain, friends in the course of the conversation asked Dan, "What was your most difficult experience during your time in Spain?" His thoughtful and painful response, "To drink my quart of milk every day and know that a child would starve because it did not have it." The relief agency had required Dan to sign a commitment that he would eat his food and drink his milk each day for his own health's sake, and to enable him to continue his ministry among the victims of the war. He kept his commitment, he said, but it was the most difficult of all his experiences—knowing that a child would starve because he drank his milk!

12
The Impossible Dream

Because of a Spanish baby who would have had forty birthdays by now, millions of people have escaped starvation and benefited from an interfaith, self-help project envisioned by Dan West in 1938.

"He could have lived had he had milk." Those words rang in Dan's ears. The baby could have lived. Its head one-third of its tiny body, its arms no bigger around than his forefinger, its loosely-covered fingers just hanging from the wrists, its eyes and cheeks sunken, and its jaw and cheek bones so prominent he scarcely noticed the skin which covered them—that baby could have lived had he had milk!

In the tiny executive office of *Gota de Leche* (Spanish for "drop of milk") Dan West looked at the waiting line of hungry babies. He saw the record of the weekly weigh-ins of one baby? 12 lbs. 3 ozs; 12 lbs. 1 oz.; 12 lb. 4 ozs.; 12 lbs. 3 ozs.; 12 lbs.; 11 lbs. 15 ozs. Only the week before those in charge had been forced to adopt the new rule that milk would no longer be given a baby who ceased to gain. Long and painful experience had persuaded them that death was only a matter of time and waiting lists were so long.

The milk which *had* saved thousands of babies in Spain that hard winter of 1937 came from Holland in great, cubical cartons of powder. Each box was emptied into a kettle and mixed with water until it had most of the nutritive and health-giving properties of the original milk. It was the best they could do, but it was not good enough. Dan knew that, for he knew that all "relief" is, in and of itself, dehumanizing. He was aware that relief must often be given, but somehow its inadequacies came upon him with crushing force as he watched the ink dry on the line that determined the fate of "Boy 123."

On the Franco side in 1937 Dan was doling out a mixture of powdered milk and water to a long line of mothers and starving children. He looked at the empty dipper in his hand, and again his heart ached. With a sip and a gulp the milk was gone and the war victim was back for more. "Surely," he thought, "there must be a better way. What good is it to fill these children's stomachs with milk for one day, only to have them return day after day or go hungry from then on?"

In January 1938, at Murcia, Spain (on the Loyalist side) he saw another long line of young and old waiting for bottles of milk. Their gaunt faces and the hopeless look in their eyes haunted him. The dying baby, the long, long lines with some sent away still hungry—what could be done to relieve the suffering of these helpless victims of a terrible war?

Sitting alone under an almond tree, Dan looked out over the grassy slopes and thought of northern Indiana where he attended college. There the people ate well and had plenty of milk. Couldn't the milk of northern Indiana be fed to the hungry in Europe? The cows could eat the green grass, produce milk for the family, and the Spanish people could then feed their own children. In that way the dependence upon relief would be overcome while all its advantages were still retained. People would have milk for their babies, but they would also have work to do—caring for the cows and milking them, and providing for future offspring. In that way more would be done than just keeping babies alive.

When Dan's term as a relief worker was completed he left Spain, going to London where he met Geoffrey Pyke, a Labor editor. The conversation naturally turned toward the starving children of Spain. Dan brought up his dream of sending cattle. Moved by Dan's story, Pyke said, "Yes, I know where you can get some cows for Spain."

"Good," Dan replied.

"But you are *not* going to send them over on the Franco side?" queried Pyke.

"Sure," answered Dan. "We must feed the hungry everywhere!"

"Well, if you're going to send even *one* cow to Franco, I won't help," Pyke concluded.

"Then," said Dan, "I'm sorry, we can't work together. In my world the needs of women and children transcend their politics."

Dan had the simple belief that a heifer is not aware of any iron or bamboo curtain and cannot distinguish between the hungry cries of communist or capitalist babies.

Returning to the United States and still dreaming, Dan brought his idea before the Committee on Spain—a group made up of representatives of the Brethren, Friends, and Mennonites—and to the Federal Council of Churches. Cows, Dan told them, would help feed families, provide fertilizer for crops and proliferate into herds. The groups were interested, but the idea did not result in any concrete plans.

He spoke cautiously to friends back home about his dream of sending cows to places where milk was needed for children. They raised questions he couldn't fully answer; they posed problems of which he was already aware; and even Lucy told him it was "an impossible dream." But Dan never gave up even though no one seemed to feel it was a practical thing to do. He persisted both inside and outside the church.

Some of Dan's Goshen neighbors who caught a glimpse of the possibilities in such a dream formed a committee, including Dan, to see what could be done. This was the first "Heifers for Relief" committee, and Dan served on it until he was incapacitated by poor health. His work was primarily that of inspiring, probing, asking why not and, in general, serving as a stimulator while others took care of the organizational procedures that have provided the successes of the project to date.

One pessimistic friend who said the "cows would never amount to anything 'over there'" agreed to take Dan to the superintendent of animal husbandry at an agricultural college nearby. While talking about the project, the professor suggested sending bred heifers. It was then that Dan envisioned another dimension to his dream, a very important one! That calf, soon to be born, could be given to another needy family, a neighbor, and soon there would be two needy families helped. By passing on the gift—on and on the gift could go. Dan believed that relief is degrading, but if you pass on what you receive it is ennobling. He was also aware that in giving we are blessed even more than in receiving. All who receive the gift of a heifer should, in turn, be givers and pass on the gift.

The entire world went to war and the starving children of Spain were forced into the background as such suffering was now multiplied a thousand-fold. Dan, who lived and suffered with the women and children of Spain, now "fought" for children everywhere.

Then in 1941 Economist Kenneth Boulding wrote an article on the economics of reconstruction which appeared in a publication of the Friends. Dan read it and felt that it provided a brand new and strengthening justification for his heifer idea. He went to the Department of Agriculture at Washington and talked with O. E. Read, chief of the Bureau of the Dairy Industry. Read was most sympathetic.

"You aren't going to sell those cows?" Read asked.

"That wasn't the idea," Dan told him. "The plan would be to give them away, just as relief food is given, but with a more permanent result."

"God bless you. If that's the idea I'll do all I can to help." Read kept that promise. For several years Dr. Read was consulted on every move. He introduced Dan to the director of the Office of Agricultural Relations, who enthusiastically endorsed the idea and brought up the possibility that the government might ship the cattle.

At a district men's meeting in Northern Indiana at Middlebury, Dan's home church, Dan was asked to present his plan of sending heifers to places where children were hungry. They not only liked the idea; they did something about it!

"I'll give a calf if someone will feed her," said Virgil Mock.

"I'll furnish the feed," volunteered O. W. Stine. "I'll feed and care for her," added his son, Claire. Two other Guernsey heifers were donated that day—one by Miss Bessie Burns and the other by the Goshen City Church of the Brethren. The three calves were named Faith, Hope, and Charity, symbols of the idea behind the gift.

Interest and support began to spread far beyond district lines. The beginning was an act of faith, for no one knew how the animals were to be delivered overseas. In June, 1942, at the Brethren Annual Conference in Asheville, North Carolina, the Brethren Service Committee approved the heifer project as part of its national program and selected a committee with Dan and a group of laymen in Northern Indiana to work out plans for securing and selecting heifers on the local church level. Andrew Cordier and Leland Brubaker of the national Brethren Service staff began meeting with the committee. It was agreed that when opportunities for relief shipments became available, the committee would ask for heifers to be sent to central points and would assume the responsibility for shipping and delivery to people in need. At this time an invitation to participate in the project was extended to people of other denominations as well.

There was no high-powered promotion, but farmers everywhere began to raise heifers for the hungry. They had a deep faith that a way for getting them to suffering people would open. This project caught the imagination of more people than anything else yet suggested as a way to respond to world hunger. Heifers were close to where many of the Brethren lived; they were basically a rural people.

Part of the proposal's success was its tangibility. It was no abstract, theological idea, but a specific, down-to-earth project they could support. Brethren were thankful that the war had not come to their shores. They had some guilt feelings that other people had suffered so much and they had been spared that suffering. They had so much materially while so many people had so little. They were eager to share. Another key to the program's success was its ongoing dimension. Each recipient of a heifer was to give the first female offspring to a needy neighbor.

Dan had the dream, but it took aggressive leadership with

organizational ability to carry it out. Soon publicity leaflets were prepared, ear tags were purchased for the gifts, a record system was set up, and other organizational trappings began to appear. John Metzler, then executive secretary of the District of Northern Indiana, Church of the Brethren, recalls quite vividly how ear tag Number One for the Hiefer Project was applied to the proper ear of the proper calf.

"Dan and I started out to tag and record the local gifts already pledged. Neither of us had any experience in ear-tagging calves, but we had the equipment and we thought reasonable intelligence. We went first to the West home, and without benefit of an audience except Dan's wife, and without any formal dedicatory service, we proceeded to apply Hiefer Project tag Number One. Dan was to do the honors on Betsy, his family's gift. The calf, small enough for us to handle with a minimum of difficulty, was tied to a fence post, and I held her head. Dan loaded the applicator pliers, placed it properly on the ear and gave it a squeeze, cutting through the ear without seeming to bother the calf very much, just a slight shake of the head. But in his inexperience and his desire to hurt as little as possible, he only half-heartedly squeezed the handle. When we examined the handiwork we found that he had cut a hole in the ear, the painful part, but did not crimp the tag through the hole. So Dan had to reapply the pliers and complete the job, which did not please the calf one bit. On tag Number Two, with the benefit of Dan's experience, I was able to complete the job with one squeeze."

By the time the first heifers had matured and were ready to be shipped, World War II had broken out. There was no possibility of shipping heifers to Spain, nor could shipping space be spared to transport heifers to the hungry any place overseas. Whether this disturbed the heifers we do not know, but it did disturb the committee. In the meantime Brethren investigation in Puerto Rico brought back stories of the need which existed there. In January, 1944, representatives of the Heifer Project Committee (HPC) and of the Farm Security Administration met and an agreement was reached—the HPC would provide for a shipment to Puerto Rico and place the cattle on the boat; the FSA would arrange and pay for shipping and distributing the heifers among the low-income farm families in Puerto Rico.

After their dedication in a worship service (which Dan attended) at the Rock Run congregation in Indiana, Faith, the first donated calf, and sixteen other bellowing Jersey, Guernsey, and Milking Shorthorn heifers, plus a calf which had already made its appearance in the world, were transported south and were swung aboard a ship at Mobile, bound for Puerto Rico, on July 14, 1944. They were the first tangible results of the most practical, realistic postwar plan devised by a United States church and probably the first shipment of its kind to leave the shores of this country. Thousands have since shared many glasses of milk with "the little people of the world."

During the war many conscientious objectors wanted to do relief work in Europe and Asia but were denied the opportunity. Instead some were sent to Castaner, Puerto Rico to open a public service project there. So Brethren boys welcomed Brethren heifers, only to discover that caring for cows in Puerto Rico, where there was no protection and little feed for the animals, was not like running a mid-west dairy farm. It was necessary for the young Brethren to become planners. One thing led to another. The cows needed shelter and feed. This demanded a higher income and better agricultural methods. Unless people were healthy and educated this could not happen. Health and education could not be achieved unless there were teachers and doctors. A call went out to teachers and doctors who then volunteered to go to Puerto Rico, and Castaner became a model community—all because a few heifers gave some people a new challenge, and others a new hope and a way to better their lives.

Faith, the Guernsey heifer tagged BSC-3, was given to Mr. Meliton Lind Lopez of Barrio Ward Mediania in the Rio Grande. She supplied milk for the family of ten children who had never tasted milk. During her lifetime she produced nine calves, including one set of twins, all of them males. At an old age she was sold for meat. Faith had several granddaughters which became a small dairy herd for Senor Lind.

The statement accompanying the shipment to the people of Puerto Rico expressed the philosophy of the gift: "These producers of nutritious milk" were being sent "to an area of great need . . . in the spirit of brotherhood and service to our fellowmen." The Brethren hoped to sustain bodies in this ministry and at the same time enrich human souls in the fellowship and love of Jesus Christ, as well as to represent in miniature the spirit of love and brotherhood which would ultimately encircle the world and embrace all nations, races, and people.

The first shipment involved 15 Guernseys, two Jerseys, and one Milking Shorthorn from Nappanee, Indiana. Records show that eleven years later, October, 1955, two of these cows were still milking, one producing 1350 pounds of milk a month and the other 1106 pounds a month. Wayne Hostetler, Heifer Project representative of Northeastern Ohio at the time, was the first "cowboy." These heifers were distributed by the Farm Security Administration and the Church of the Brethren representatives. The FSA complimented the Brethren on their excellent stock and humanitarian gesture of goodwill; the Brethren were well satisfied with the distribution of the heifers to poor families who owned no dairy cattle.

This was the beginning of a worldwide, interfaith, self-help project known today as Heifer Project International (HPI).

The idea of Heifers for Relief continued to spread through Brethren communities in Indiana, Ohio, Pennsylvania, Maryland, Virginia, and on west through Illinois and Iowa to California. Kermit Eby noted that by 1945 the project needed a full-time director. That person was Ben Bushong, a Pennsylvania dairy farmer who knew cattle and the Brethren. He soon learned about international politics. Ben observed that "There is no red tape that cannot be cut—and people are always more important than brass." Ben used to joke about the first heifers for Europe—which turned out to be "Six bulls to Greece."

The Brethren Service Committee (later the Brethren Service Commission) was eager to secure the cooperation of government agencies such as the United Nations Relief and Rehabilitation Administration (UNRRA), whose policies were still in the formative stage. Dan had some misgivings about working with government agencies, but he recognized that "we are trying to do a clean job in a dirty world." He wanted the Heifer Project Committee "to have a frank, honest policy which does not involve us politically more than is necessary with any government." He had faced this problem in Spain, and he was afraid that the church would face a continuing problem if it worked with the governmental agencies such as UNRRA. One of the problems was distribution. Would the cattle be given to UNRRA for distribution? The committee insisted that Brethren must give the heifers directly to the people in need. With the promise of a mutually satisfactory management, Brethren were encouraged to continue collecting heifers for shipment.

In June, 1945, UNRRA asked the HPC to supply "seagoing cowboys" to care for the livestock which UNRRA planned to ship overseas. The Brethren accepted the challenge to secure the thousands of men that UNRRA wanted. By August 21, 1946, four-thousand eight-hundred thirty-nine men from various churches or from no church had sailed with cattle for places around the world. UNRRA was happy to accept for shipment all the animals which the Brethren could gather.

Dan was pleased with Bushong's relationship with UNRRA for he helped to determine their policies, which was the way Dan felt the Brethren ought to work with the power state. UNRRA's program was in some ways patterned after the pioneering venture of the Brethren. The Heifer Project was recognized as one of the finest relief projects; thousands of Brethren men, old and young, saw the suffering war caused and gained a world outlook as well.

As the project grew it became necessary to collect shipment-ready animals in local communities so that truckers, contributing their services, could load them easily. Then, larger collection center-farms were established and equipped so the animals could be tested. Veterinarians frequently contributed their services and cleared the shipping papers before the animals were sent to port for shipment. The headquarters for the Heifer Project was established near New Windsor after the Brethren had purchased a complex of former college buildings to be used as a relief center.

A blow to the project came when UNRRA ended in 1947. The Brethren had over 700 heifers, about ready to freshen, collected on 24 farms but no shipping space was now available. Some cattle were sold with funds being used to purchase replacements when shipment again became possible; some were returned to their donors. Ben Bushong wouldn't take no for an answer even from the most powerful, so, with persistence, occasionally a ship was secured.

In the meantime, however, another significant opportunity for the project developed. As a result of the Yalta and Potsdam agreements in 1945, following the war, the Eastern European countries were permitted to expel all people of German descent. Some twelve-million people were forced to leave their homes and migrate to refugee camps in Germany. The postwar West German government made immediate plans to handle the refugee problem by purchasing land and building homes, then selling them to the refugees, mostly farmers, on long-term, low-interest loans. Heifer Project was invited to assist this group and for a period of eight years shipments of fifty to sixty-five animals were sent at six-week intervals using the hold of the ship known to hundreds of "seagoing cowboys" as the S. S. American Importer.

An office for distribution was established at Kassel House, a center in Kassel, Germany which the Brethren had set up for a relief and rehabilitation program in that area. It was staffed largely by Brethren Volunteer Service workers. The distribution of twenty-one heifers to German refugees was one of the highlights of the festivities commemorating the denomination's observance of its 250th anniversary in 1958, held in Germany, the country of its origin.

When Heifer Project celebrated the presentation of its 9,000th cow to one of the West German refugees, the farmer put his arm over the neck of the brown and white purebred. "Thank you," he told the young American Brethren worker standing nearby. "May God bless you for this gift." Turning to his wife the refugee, filled with emotion, spoke almost in a whisper: "Trudy, we have a cow to give us milk for the children, cheese for the pantry, butter for our bread. With our American cow we can start a new life in Germany. From this cow we can build a new herd." The refugee, stripped of his possessions by the Communists, had been kicked around so long he found it hard to believe somebody actually wanted to help him to a new life.

Among historic events of that period was a shipment of cattle to the Soviet Union in 1956. Thurl Metzger, the director of the Heifer Project at that time, joined the "seagoing cowboys" (Milo Yoder, Mark Schrock, and Paul Miller) and their charges upon their arrival in Russia as guests of the Ministry of Agriculture. Though this was a period of political tension, they were graciously received, giving credence to M. R. Zigler's statement, "You can go anywhere on the back of a heifer."

As the program became increasingly well-known, developing nations began to request help from Heifer Project. This presented a new problem. Shipping cattle to Europe was a simple case of giving quality animals to experienced farmers. But in the developing nations, where the Heifer Project operates almost exclusively now, there is need to provide know-how along with the animals. Thus, the program today has changed from relief and rehabilitation to development, requiring new procedures and techniques. The purpose is the same as that originally conceived by Dan West and implemented by the first committee—to help those in need regardless of race, creed, or politics and in a way that will permit them to share the increase.

In 1953, this Church of the Brethren enterprise, was incorporated as an independent, non-profit organization. The headquarters was established in October, 1971, at Little Rock, Arkansas to be near the newly purchased Fourche Ranch. Today regional offices are located in Plymouth, Massachusetts; Goshen, Indiana, which had just recently built a new office; and in Monrovia and Modesto, California.

A big step was taken in September, 1971, when Heifer Project, Inc. purchased the 1200-acre Fourche Ranch, near Perryville, Ark. This International Livestock Center is used as a receiving facility for donated animals and serves also as a staging area for livestock shipments, and for a breeding herd of 500 purebred Angus and Brangus cows as well as other animals, such as pigs, sheep, and goats. Soon after the purchase of the ranch—for $750,000 with no money down and a 20-year mortgage—the name was changed to Heifer Project International.

HPI was able to pay off the loan on the ranch in six years. During the same period the HPI program values increased from about $1 million in 1971 to more than $2.5 million in 1976. On July 2, 1977, the mortgage burning ceremony took place on the ranch. Part of the celebration was the dedication of large tracts of acres funded by various church groups and service organizations, including the Dan West Acres, 52 acres given by friends of the founder of Heifer Project. Lucy West, Dan's widow, was among those attending the ceremony. Placed on a large boulder near the main building of the project is a plaque engraved with these words:

DAN WEST ACRES
honoring
Dan West, 1893-1971
Founder of Heifer Project
Ambassador of Peace
Neighbor to the World
"He loved God and made a
career of helping others."

Reflecting on the change in approach but not the purpose, Ed Geers, HPI's former executive director said, "Men and women want to be actors, not spectators, in their own liberation from poverty . . . unless persons feel that they can grow as human beings, can grow as masters of their own development and share in decisions, no amount of material effort will achieve liberation. Development—the process of freeing humanity from the constraints of hunger, disease, and utter dependence on ill-understood natural forces—must be human if it is to be successful." To that end the organization, in its 33-year history, has been responsible for placing over 50,000 animals and over 1½ million chickens with needy persons in over 90 countries and more than 20 states in the USA.

Heifer Project still insists that whenever an animal is placed, the recipient agree that the first female offspring of that gift animal be given to another needy family which is properly trained in animal husbandry to care for it adequately. "Solving the problem of hunger one family at a time," says Geer, "is a trademark of the Heifer Project approach."

Almost anywhere one travels HPI can be seen in action. In Ecuador a big Boeing 707 flies in with a cargo of pigs; in Zaire a little single-engine Cessna touches down on a bumpy grass strip bringing day-old chicks to a village in Kwilu province. In India it might be a shipload of rambouillet sheep or goats; in Panama, bees; in the Dominican Republic, dairy cows. And so it goes, the year round. Heifer Project workers know where to find a certain kind of animal and how to arrange shipping details so that it will arrive at some remote point in the world in good time and in good condition. Shipping instructions once called for transporting 624 chicks from a hatchery near Pittsburgh, PA to a small community in northern Greece. The chicks were crated, taken to the Pittsburgh airport by truck, flown to Newark, transferred by helicopter to Idlewild, flown to Rome, transferred to another plane, flown to Athens, and hauled by jeep over 200 miles of mountain roads. Not one chick was lost!

A bishop in Crete watched the assortment of Heifer Project animals disembark from the plane that had brought them to his island parish. "I thought it was something like the moment right after the biblical flood when the animals started coming out to fill the new world," he said with a chuckle.

From its unpretentious beginning, the heifer idea has grown to staggering statistical proportions. But HPI personnel prefer to cite examples of self-help rather than point to the various totals.

For example:

• In South Korea, 50 percent of the present chicken population is descended from HPI chicks and hatching eggs.

• In Iran, where 14 years ago 50 purebred cattle were sent to upgrade local stock, an estimated 90,000 cross-breeds are now producing three times as much milk as native cows.

• In Ecuador, a sow which can produce as much as two tons of meat in a year from her litters can double a family's income; in the Philippines, HPI pigs grow four times as fast as the local breeds.

• In India, cross-breeding with bulls furnished by HPI has produced offspring which are tripling previous milk production figures because the cows mature in eighteen months rather than the previous three or four years. That success has prompted the World Bank to loan $30 million to organize small farmers in 1,800 dairy cooperatives.

Former recipients become donors. To project headquarters there came recently $37,500 from West Germany's *Evangelische Hilfswerk* (Protestant) and *Caritas* (Catholic) relief agencies—allotted from their *"Brot fur die Welt"* campaign. The money was designated for shipment of animals to India. Japan has sent goats and rabbits to Korea. The Philippines has sent hatching eggs to Vietnam. Iran, Turkey, and Greece have sent eggs and chicks to Jordan. It's contagious!

A spin-off of the HPI projects in India is an Australian program "For Those Who Have Less." While visiting India, a member of the Australian Parliament once asked Prime Minister Nehru what his country could do to assist India. Nehru pointed out the successes of HPI, and the Australian counterpart came into being. The Down Under continent has since branched out and now is performing this helpful service in other areas of the world.

"A Gift of Life Is a Gift of Love." These words, printed in large letters, greet you as you drive up the road to the entrance of HPI. They ring true as you tour the ranch and talk with its dedicated staff. As one member confessed: "I formerly looked at our help merely as providing animals for those in need. Recently, I've come to see more—it also gives new meaning to life for those who share with others through the giving of the animals."

The Dan West Education Fund, established as a memorial to the founder of HPI, is to be used to support volunteers who manifest his spirit and who are able to give training in animal husbandry to recipients of HPI livestock. Such persons are needed, insists Thurl Metzger, the Director of International Programs. Writing in *Sharing Life,* the HPI newsletter, Metzger says, "HPI representatives have an overwhelming opportunity and responsibility. They must gain the confidence of the poor and the respect of the powerful. In addition to being technically qualified they should reflect 'the fruits of the spirit which are love, joy, peace, long-suffering, gentleness, goodness, faith, meekness and temperance,' plus a good sense of humor." These qualities "manifest Dan's spirit," whose gentle voice was rarely raised except when he talked about the accomplishment of HPI. Then he really got excited. "Too much has already been said as if I were responsible for this." he exclaimed. "The credit belongs to God and should be given to him. It was God in the hearts of farmers who actually raised the heifers and in the hearts of the many, many people who have helped."

"Yes," responded an interviewer, "and God in the heart of a man who listened for the voice of God in the whispering grass and the wailing babies and the sobbing mothers."

Upon Dan's death, Thurl Metzger said, "The church has lost a prophet, the cause of peace has lost a champion, and millions around the world have lost a friend. Dan's allegiance was always to the common people," continued Metzger, the man who helped translate Dan's ideals into the ongoing programs of Heifer Project. "Dan refused to eat cake until all could have their daily bread."

Kermit Eby wrote that "Heifers, unlike bombs, are personal, particularly if you bring them up or sacrifice for them. Before they mature and become cows (giving their new host not only milk but the beginnings of a dairy herd) they become pets. Sent away to help the needy, a part of you goes along. Received by fellowmen in need, the Fatherhood of God and the brotherhood of man is reaffirmed.

"And so once more the word became flesh; and brotherhood takes on meaning because first a simple Brethren dreamer and than a church realized that brotherhood knew no boundaries."

13
Proposals and Programs

Three other important movements developed as by-products of the relief program for Spain: (1) work camps, volunteer service, and alternative service; (2) gifts in kind; and (3) the resettlement of war refugees in America. Though Dan was involved in helping to initiate and work out all the programs, the work camp and volunteer programs were his main arenas of activity.

Upon his return from Spain, Dan realized that the work camp efforts to help people in our own country were quite similar to relief programs abroad. Two work camps were planned for the summer of 1939, as an increasing number of youth were considering giving at least one year of their lives toward preventing war and building peace.

Dan dreamed of a combined effort on the part of all Christian groups, all those who wanted to help *in peace time,* to develop volunteer programs similar to work camps. If the church had such a program and war came, he reasoned, permission might be granted for the church to continue its work under civilian, not military, control. If the church got busy on jobs such as these, it would have earned its right to ask for exemption from military service. Its record would offer a better argument to show its sincerity than its intentions. Dan's creative proposals played a considerable part in developing the church's relationship to Selective Service during World War II and even later in the 1950s.

At the Brethren Annual Conference in Colorado Springs in 1948, an idea planted by Dan was given a big push by the young people in attendance. Urged on by some peace caravaners, they went directly to the floor of conference with a proposal recommending that a broad plan of volunteer service be instituted for Brethren youth, especially for those of conscription age, *at once.* The youth wanted the church to speed up its peace programs *now!*

A query dealing with the peace question had just been rejected by the conference delegates. A small group of youth decided something should be done. As one girl walked down the aisle to leave the auditorium, she slapped Dan on the arm and said, "We need you." It was impossible for him to refuse a request like that even though he had been a bit conservative in his earlier advice to the youth. He followed her to a back room where a handful of young people had started working on a new plan. Out of it Brethren Volunteer Service (BVS) was born.

To the credit of the older Brethren the new query just hatched up by the youth was given consideration and kind treatment. Minds were open to the new idea as Ted Chambers, standing on a soap box to give him enough extra height to reach the microphone and be seen, presented the essential outline of the plan for BVS. Conference accepted the plan.

"At no Annual Meeting which this writer has attended have I seen the youth take so active a part or receive such warm receptiveness. The Brethren are back of their youth in this crisis," reported the editor of *The Gospel Messenger.*

One youth reported the excitement generated by the action at the Annual Conference: "I went to my first Annual Conference in Colorado Springs in 1948 and saw BVS born. Following the conference I went to a two-week camp with Dan and Ted Chambers as leaders. This was a whole new dimension of church life I was experiencing. Dan challenged us to be as serious in our Christian commitment as the Communists were in their cause. He talked about discipline, things as they ought to be, a world perspective on problems, and about simplifying our own lives. ... This kind of thinking and challenging was refreshing and stimulating to me. I committed a year to BVS, came home and resigned my teaching position, and took off for training in September."

The initial response to Brethren Volunteer Service was overwhelming. The Brethren Service Commission office received stacks of mail, telephone calls, and visits from church officials, pastors, parents, young people, and others who were interested in helping to develop and participate in the program. The BSC staff, with Dan as a member, worked hard in planning and organizing a program which began in September of that year.

Its beginning was not without criticism, but by 1951 BVS was sufficiently recognized that it was accepted as a possible form of alternative service for all men who sought conscientious objector status and were ordered into alternative service by their draft boards. Dan's dream of what could happen if "we earn the right to ask for exemption from military duty" became a reality.

While Dan continually raised expectations about what could and should happen in the world, he did not offer false hopes or give false assurances. His probing and his questioning seemed to challenge people to think positively—for conditions and people to change means commitment and work. Dan was a bridge between young and old. He was a bridge between the "little" Brethren and the so-called "big wheels" in the church.

Dan needs to be understood in the light of the problems of the times in which he lived. His emphasis on the "little" people, on doing your own thinking, on not being overwhelmed by "big" people in the church or in government—these ideas were needed then. They do not seem revolutionary now, but in the 40s when people were awed by a government that could come in and draft their sons for war or for military training after the war was over, and when the "little" people were in some awe of leaders in the denomination—in this period Dan's message was relevant.

Among the mementos of one volunteer was a prayer Dan gave in a Peace Workshop in 1948:

Our Father, we thank thee that we are living now in thy troubled world.

We thank thee for the hard problems we don't know how to solve yet.

We thank thee for the faith that dares to try to solve them.

We thank thee for our Lord and Master, thy Son, who can show us the way.

Wilt thou look on all we have done and bless whatever is good;

And wilt thou help us to antidote what is not good;

And wilt thou make of us more profitable servants for Jesus' sake. Amen.

The second movement growing out of the Spanish Civil War relief project was the sharing of gifts-in-kind, in addition to gifts of money, for the relief of human suffering. "In a world at war, clothing does more than warm the bodies of those who receive it; it warms the heart." Brethren searched their closets, sewed garments and bought blankets to send abroad. Seeing the benefits of involving "grass roots" people in this way, Dan supported proposals that material be collected in a central area, packed and shipped to areas of need. Dan and others were keenly aware of the long-range possibilities of such a program. The result of this specific kind of relief program was the creation of Church World Service on May 7, 1946, the integration into one organization of three agencies that had been serving churches in America. Some leaders outside the Church of the Brethren denomination have speculated that CWS might not have happened without the Brethren.

A third outgrowth of the Spanish Civil War, plus the additional unrest in Europe, was the project of resettling European refugees in America. In September 1931, Dan recommended that between fifty and two hundred European refugees be brought to the U. S. by June, 1939. Little was done to implement Dan's suggestion then, but later local churches were urged to place refugee families from war areas in their communities. From that time to this refugees from many countries have found a home through such programs. Dan's idea of "getting to know you" was another attempt to bring world peace and at the same time witness to the faith of the Brethren and their belief in world peace.

Besides all the programs Dan was initiating and promoting, he continued to speak forcefully for peace by advocating pacifism and nonresistance. In Spain he had witnessed the misery, suffering, and anguish that was imposed on people; the havoc, plunder, and general destruction to property, and the ravage and devastation of the earth itself. He was convinced that war must never happen again—anywhere. Understanding, goodwill, and love were the answers!

In an article, "A Look at Some of My Values," written in October, 1938, Dan pointed out that persons everywhere have many values: life, family, personal possessions, one's country and Christ's way of life. Dan wrote that Jesus had much to say about rightness and justice, but he had more to say about love. Jesus commanded us to love our enemies. It is easy to trick ourselves at this point, he said. Twenty years ago a professor in a theological school prayed that "our soldiers might kill German soldiers in the spirit of love." "Christianity had better not be mentioned in that business," Dan insisted.

Continuing, Dan suggested: "Millions of people on this earth also have all these values. The important thing is, which comes first when we cannot have them all. In peace time, our time and energy tend to be spent on ourselves, our families, and our property. . . . But when crisis comes . . . our values are oriented from other centers. Then we know that we have something bigger to live for; sometimes so much bigger that our own comfort, our property, and even our lives are risked—and sometimes lost—in a greater cause. . . .

"Some Christians' values have shifted recently. Some who were pacifists three years ago insist that Spain has made things different; next China, and now Czechoslovakia. They would fight for justice and kill their fellowmen in the name of all they consider holy. The real determiner may be a philosophic value they hope to save—democracy or whatever—by surrendering their Christian way of life. . . . For all non-Christians the Fatherland can well come first, but for Christians it can *never* be first."

Though also committed to international peace, a friend of Dan's differed with the means Dan advocated for obtaining it.

While Dan felt that peace could be secured through love, the historian believed that peace could be obtained only through political institutions.

In an article, this proponent of peace suggested that war is an instrument for making adjustments, used by practically no one willingly. But as conditions become progressively unsatisfactory more and more people feel that war, bad as it may be, is preferable to a continuation of the present situation.

In answer to the question he anticipated would be raised—Can the use of coercion by the great majority when things get unbearable be squared with the church's doctrine of nonresistance?—he cited the statement of Jesus. If personal attempts at adjustment fail, then the matter is to be submitted to the church and if that, too, fails, then the offender may be separated from the church. The church has used coercive measures quite extensively, and the authority for it is good, he maintained.

This critic felt there are many evidences of spiritual maturity—humility, mercy, purity of heart, honesty, justice—but the Brethren have overemphasized nonresistance. The church has a nobler function than a stubborn protest against violence as a way of adjustment. Its peace program is not wrong, but it needs a positive program, the prevention of war.

Dan's later statements reveal that he took such criticism seriously. "I am grateful that that little remnant did not let go of their "No" to war . . . but we have done little to build for peace between wars; we have chiefly objected to wars. Our 'No' unfortunately has been louder than our 'Yes' . . . . We need now to compensate by learning what 'Yes' to a brave new world means. . . . We must out-sacrifice—out-live—out-die the soldiers if we are to merit hearing. . . . I am still looking for a group which will give as much for peace as a soldier gives for war. . . . "

The cooperation of the Brethren Service Committee and the United States government reached a new point in relations of church and state in the development of Civilian Public Service camps.

With the drafting of conscientious objectors under the Selective Service Act of 1940 and the subsequent entry of

America into World War II, the provision of an adequate alternative service program for those who accepted the status of conscientious objectors became an increasing concern. With the possibility that the government would be willing to provide technical assistance, tools, equipment, and unused Civilian Conservation Corps camps, the Brethren with the Friends and the Mennonites each agreed to provide such camps for their young men and immediately began planning. The first Civilian Public Service camp was opened at Lagro, Indiana in May, 1941.

Some Brethren leaders, including Dan, felt that the church had been forced into the role of "junior partner" with Selective Service as the "senior partner." Though Dan was not in full agreement with the arrangement, in 1943, he agreed to be the director of the School of Pacifist Living at Cascade Locks, Oregon, another of the CPS camps. All enrollees in the school made a commitment of at least eight hours of study per week above the fifty-one hours on the work project.

Reports of the twelve study groups reveal the leadership of Dan and his belief that pacifism meant more than conscientious objection to war—to him it was a way of life! The men studied pacifist living in the home, outside the home, in face-to-face groups, and in community activities. Included also were the economic implications of pacifist living; pacifism and world problems; pacifist living and education; nonresistance, "second-mile" nonviolence; the philosophical bases of pacifism; disciplines necessary for pacifist living; pacifist lessons from history; the relation of pacifism to government and functional democracy; and pacifist living and the class struggle.

Except for the government's involvement in the CPS program, Dan was pleased that the church offered humanitarian alternatives to going to war.

Many young men, faced with the draft, struggled with Dan's six levels of conscience which he graphically presented in church after church: (1) no conscience, join military; (2) willingness to kill to right what was wrong; (3) noncombatant service in the military (IAO); (4) deferment, allowed by the government for ministers, and persons in industry vital to the war effort; (5) no deferment, willing to make choice and live with it; and (6) say "No," *love all people,* and be willing to suffer the consequences.

After the discussion, Dan expressed his own personal feelings—"Everyone who feels he can't kill is a friend of mine. If conscientious, he's a brother of mine. Beneath our levels of action we must have Christ and conscience. This is dynamic; it moves men up!"

Dan's very positive assertions about peace, the draft, and status when drafted were not always accepted; and at times some people expressed animosity towards him. If a Brethren chose to go into the army, navy or marine corps, many felt he was still a part of the church and should be ministered to and accepted by his fellow church members. Dan's convictions were strong that a person should have no part in the military. Even noncombatant service was unacceptable to him. One minister was criticized by Dan for conducting a funeral service in the church for a fellow who was killed while serving as a CO in the army. Here was a conflict between two of Dan's strongest principles. While he believed implicitly in the acceptance of each person regardless of his beliefs, Dan, at that time in history, did not feel that the church should minister to anyone who chose military service.

Apparently Dan mellowed, for in the *Youth Fellowship Manual* (1953) he wrote: "We hold steady as a pacifist church and aim to grow stronger in the doctrine. But we do not compel the consciences of our members. Alexander Mack (the founder of the Church of the Brethren) recommended 'No force in religion.' And so we do not throw out members who joined the armed forces. This is a hard position to hold also."

On one card found among his files, a variety of interesting notes were listed: appointments at the university at 10:30 a.m. and again at 3 p.m.; the call numbers of five books in the 100s and 200s (philosophy and religion). Also included on the card was a quotation by Robert C. Calhoun: "Our concern is not to obscure or to obliterate differences but to set them in clearer, truer light so that each of us may learn from his neighbor, and our differences, purged of arrogance and error, may come to enrich, not to isolate, the unity we affirm."

"The unity we affirm." Dan believed this unity could bring about brotherhood as a reality—free from hate and war, with love and serving one's neighbor as the unifying force of the entire world.

Unity! Peace! It could happen, Dan believed. "Peace on earth" was more than a cliche at Christmas; for Dan it was his continuing dream. War was as horrible to one small child as it was to Dan. Dan's sensitivity to the child's fear is illustrated in the story of Butch.

At the opening of a peace institute in 1947, Dan showed a vivid technicolor sound film, "The Way to Peace." Because it ended a bit too horribly for the children he saw in the audience, Dan cut the film short.

As Dan was discussing the problems of peace, he noticed that eight-year old Butch, sitting on the front row, was beginning to cry. First Butch went to his father, then to his mother, sobbing all the time and looking up at Dan as he spoke. Finally, his mother took him out.

When the meeting was over, Dan learned from Butch's parents, in whose home he stayed that night, that Butch cried because the threat of war bothered him very much. Feeling a deep obligation toward Butch, Dan talked with him the next morning. After their conversation, Dan went to his room and wrote this report and gave it to Butch.

"Butch, tell me why you cried last night."

"I don't like to hear about war. It was that picture and some of the things you said."

"Well, Butch, I don't want to make things any rosier than they are, but I'm trying to work so there won't be any war."

"Well, I'm not so much afraid of war, but we live close to the bomb place [Sunnyside is about 50 miles from Hanford, Wash.] and that might blow up sometime. Then at school the bigger boys talk about Russia, and it makes me scared."

"Do they talk about it often?"

"Oh, pretty often. I know that not everything they say is true, but it scares me anyway."

"Did you sleep all right last night?"

"Sure, I nearly always do."

"That's good. You see, I'm trying to help, and a lot of

other people are trying to help, keep away from war, and I believe we can do it if we work hard. Then you won't be scared anymore, will you?"

"I'm not scared this morning. I thought how we can keep from having a war—send missionaries."

"We ought to send a lot of missionaries. The more we send, the surer there won't be any war."

"What do you think you'll be when you grow up, Butch?"

"I think I'll be a missionary or a preacher."

The note went on: "Butch and millions of other boys and girls his age are afraid of the future. It's the job of Christians all over the world to shift their attention in the direction of the Kingdom of God on earth. If we can do that, we can have peace."

Ten years later, April 10, 1957, in a speech given at Ashland Seminary in Ashland, Ohio, Dan listed six key statements "for us to think about":

1. There is no Christian way to kill a man.

2. If the Christians in the world would refuse to kill each other, there would be no war.

3. If you respect personality, you cannot kill men.

4. Human life is sacred. Life isn't a "thing."

5. If you take action against war, it must be for conscience' sake.

6. The Christian's job is to give maximum witness to his faith.

Then he ended the speech, "There are many things a Christian can do that are 'constructive' rather than 'destructive' for his country. These activities, such as working in slum areas, hospitals, and missions are much better than learning to hate and kill other people. Jesus said, 'Love your neighbor.' Killing him and bringing suffering to his family are poor ways to show love!"

14
A Spring Wound Tight

In an article, "Radicals Now?" Dan suggested that the church had been chiefly conservative in doctrine due largely to following closely the teachings of the New Testament and living in comparative isolation from the rest of the world. In practice, however, Brethren had not been that traditional. "This is attributable," he wrote, "to the great lag between ideals and living, common to the run of men. . . . Hypocrites cannot be happy, and we cannot live in compartments when the world is rough. Either our doctrines will determine our practice or vice versa. The latter possibility has the inside track for we live our way into our thinking more than we think our way into living."

As the four sons and one daughter in the West family grew older they became increasingly aware of some duplicity and ambivalence in their father's life. Whether Dan realized this lag between ideals and living we do not know. But one of the ironies of his life is that as the initiator of the Hilltop experiences in the late 30s and as a trainer of sensitivity in human relation labs in the 40s and a leader in Mission 12, their successor in the late 50s, Dan's relationship with his wife and children continued to remain somewhat stilted and aloof. He seemed reluctant to be vulnerable—to expose his feeling.

The children wished he would "get down off his moralistic high horse," as they used to say, and "join humanity for a while"—to be just their father, a human person with more feelings toward them. Instead it seemed that he treated them as expendables or as part of an experiment for his dream world of the ideal. It was as if his wife and children were actors in his great design, as he once told one of the children, a design which was somewhat circumscribed by the church at that time. It seemed important to him to be able to talk with people in churches, camps, and various meetings about his wife and five children. Somehow the image of himself as a family man was central to his message of simple living, of Christian living, or of his dream for the future. His children would be better than he; their world would be better than his.

To the five he seemed married to the church, as if he were trying to make the church and the family one. When Dan taught a youth Sunday school class at Middlebury, Indiana he made it quite interesting (though half of the class might be his own children), but his tone of voice and the language he used were much the same as when he conducted family councils. It seemed to the children that he tried more to make them like ideal church members than to help them discover how they were human and how to handle feelings they had as children and later as adults. He couldn't seem to relax with them because he could not refrain from giving them some moral lesson regardless of their age. He gave a moral twist to each thing they did, to something they read, reported on, or saw. This is not surprising when one stops to think about it. He had dedicated his life so completely to Christ, to the church, to the betterment of society. He did not marry until he was almost thirty-nine, and their last child was born when he was almost fifty. The church was, and continued to be, his life.

One can imagine, too, what it might be like to be admired for your idealism and your prophetic vision while traveling throughout the churches and then be dropped suddenly into another world—the world of reality, home. Children, five of them, were living and enjoying the *now*. Dreams of the ideal can quickly be shattered and challenged by their realism. Dan's emphasis on long-term consequences, though later appreciated, seemed irrelevant and tedious then. His dreams for the future seemed "out of this world." The generation gap is hard enough to deal with when parents are younger, but to be sixty and an idealist made family life, and his life, even more difficult.

Some questions go unanswered. Why did Dan who had once "hated the culture which produced him" not identify more closely with his children and the atmosphere in which he was raising them? Why, when he talked about individual needs and the uniqueness of each person, did he seem to use pressure to pour each member of his family into the "Dan West" mold? And, why, when he taught the children to think, to read, to study, to evaluate, was he so reluctant to see them grow up and grow away from him?

He seemed to see them all as crumbling, instead of relishing their becoming independent of him. To the children it was a narrow way of watching growth and changes which are inevitable in people and in the times. The 60s brought out the rebellions of many people against society; and Dan, it appeared, saw all this as a nightmare. He became a bit cynical about his view of the world, a traumatic blow to a man who had been so optimistic, so sure the world and people would get better and better if "we" just worked hard enough. It is no doubt fortunate that Dan did not live to see two of his sons divorced. It might have been very difficult for him to have handled those family crises.

In their early years the West children found it hard to establish their identity and independence. At school they did not say the pledge of allegiance to the flag or learn nationalistic songs. Permission was withheld for several years for the boys to participate in competitive sports because of the similarities between them and the military. When the twins were sophomores in high school they were allowed to play basketball even though their older brother had wanted to but was denied the opportunity. They were a bit resentful that they were not as good as the other players because of their late start.

For Steve, the youngest, the sports situation was more hurtful. It was agreed that he would go out for basketball on a trial basis until Christmas to see if he could get everything done, including the chores at home. Steve wasn't able to complete all the tasks around the farm, so a family discussion was held. It was a tearful session when the decision that Steve could no longer play on the team was reached. Basketball had been very important to him. Through it he had developed a sense of self-respect which had been hard to achieve when growing up with three older brothers and an older sister. Steve did play his sophomore and senior years (he was traveling his junior year) but he, too, had lost some early basic training which would have made him a much better player. The permission, finally, to play showed that Dan could be flexible when he was convinced that he needed to be.

It seemed especially hard for Dan to see their daughter, Jan, grow up. Jan wanted to cut her hair, but Dan felt, from reading in the Bible, that short hair on women connoted a bad impression. Jan took the initiative and cut off one of her long braids. There was no comment from her mother except that the other one would have to be cut off or she would look ridiculous. Lipstick was another issue. Had it not been for an understanding mother the girl in the family would have had a rough time.

Dating was another difficult phase in growing up. Chaperones were never known well enough to be satisfactory to their father. Cheerleaders, showing off their bodies, could in no way be good girls. Many of the puritanical standards imposed on the children made life embarrassing when they were with their peers. The admonition of their father, "It's important, you know, that the morning after a date you should be able to look your date in the eye," and "keep an arm's length from her," irritating to them, was part of Dan's philosophical view that dating was primarily one of verbal interaction.

Dan and Lucy had dreams for the family. At one time they wanted the boys to form a barbershop quartet as her brothers had done. Then Dan thought it would be good for the boys to form a clinic similar to the Menningers in Topeka, Kansas. It was also Dan's hope that one of his boys would take over the farm. He wanted the continuity of the farm passing from father to son. This was never realized. The farm has been sold, except for about twenty-five acres of the land which is nothing but woods, woods which were decimated by a tornado in 1965.

After the children learned to swim, Dan urged Lucy to

learn also, for some day, he dreamed, they would all canoe down the Danube together, but that wouldn't be possible until Lucy could swim. They didn't make it to Europe as an intact family but they did start out as one on a trip to Eugene, Oregon in 1956, for the Annual Conference.

To parents with five tall children ranging in age from 13 to 22 this must have been an enormous undertaking. Delays in Nebraska to fix the overdrive of the old Nash and unbearably hot weather had made them irritable travelers, but as they came into the mountains west of Laramie, Wyoming the trip picked up interest. The next day at noon, Larry was performing his little ritual of jumping over every picnic table in the area.

It was a consequential jump. Landing in a spiral turn, he broke his leg in several places. Lucy, emptying some trash, saw Larry on the ground. Evidently thinking he had been shot when she heard the bone crack, she, too, fell to the ground. Jan went over to her. Dan came to Larry's aid. "Dad took command in a marvelous way," commented Larry. "I felt tremendously secure as I laid on the ground with a crooked leg that was most painful." Phil called the ambulance and after X-rays, Dan, Phil, Jan and Larry drove 150 miles from Lander, over the mountains, to Casper, using the Nash Rambler as a do-it-yourself ambulance. Surgery the next day proved successful and another trip back to Lander brought Lucy, Steve and Joel. Lucy decided to remain with Larry until he was ready to leave the hospital and then ride the train home with him. Dan took the other four, made it to Eugene, and gave the speech which had been assigned to Lucy.

After a good time with friends at Conference, the five traveled down through California. At one point it was raining and the children begged their father to let them stay in a motel. "No, no," Dan said, "it's not raining that hard." So they camped among the sequoias with the rain falling gently around them. To cook their meal they had to bend over a tree to keep the water from splashing in the pan. No one remembers how they got the fire started, but they fried up a batch of fish and warmed a can of beans. Result, a delicious meal! They managed to camp dry that night and continued their trip on down to San Francisco. It seemed their father took charge in an emergency or on trips in a marvelous way. He didn't give up easily on a challenge, such as Larry's accident or the rain. That was one of the things they all admired about him.

When they had been younger, Annual Conferences were not as pleasant as this one. The children became restless waiting for Dan while he talked with people. Such trips were business trips, not fun or vacation trips for the rest of the family. Though the youngsters did put in time by sliding down the bannisters of the hotel at Colorado Springs or by going swimming at Richmond, they had to wait around for Dan. After meetings he shook hands and talked with people, getting a lot of mileage out of it personally, the children thought, and perhaps it was for the good of the church. But when you're young and hungry and bored, time can drag on and on.

College years brought out even more rebellion. At Manchester College, their parents' alma mater, the four oldest tried to prove that they were persons in their own right. A rebellion against the church and the past was one way; dating unapproved girls and boys was another. Going to Oberlin for his college work was the youngest's way of making it on his own. The use of profanity in their letters to each other, which Dan discovered when he opened some of them, was another reaction against the strict puritanism they had known as children.

Some rebelled more than others but all did it in rather colorful and dramatic ways, each in his or her own way. They were hungry for all kinds of freedom. The spring had been wound too tightly; something had to give. Rebellion was the way for them, as it was and continues to be for many young persons.

Brilliant and inquiring minds, urged to seek further education and knowledge, to analyze and make evaluations, and then to arrive at their own decisions, do not remain provincial nor necessarily like their parents. Dan had taught them well to take a stance, to argue for it, and to defend it. Since he wanted them to do that he had to accept somehow where they came out. But it must have shocked Dan to see his children create new values for themselves for he deeply believed that he had a good system of training for his family. To the question posed in an article, "Shall we try to keep our young people safe in the nest, making them believe exactly as we do?" he could no longer answer "No" as he had in 1931. By 1950 his honest answer had to be "I tried by imposing my value system on them." His method had resulted in a pinning down of very strong and free spirits which ultimately had to break out. Their parents must have pondered, as parents have through the ages, "Where did we fail?"

It is interesting that Dan could not see that his children were doing much the same thing, but in a different way, as the young people who followed him. These youth were, in a sense, already uprooted from some secure but stifling environment. This was the reason they became involved in work camps, peace seminars, Hilltops. They, too, were hungry for some new thinking, often ready to change. Somehow Dan did not seem to realize that he challenged the thinking of the children of other parents, upsetting the status quo and their ideas for their children. These children had rebelled and left the security of their more conservative backgrounds to engage in activities which were likewise revolutionary in their parents' eyes.

While some hurts and scars remain in the West children, time and maturity have been healing and will continue to heal. They were able to acquire freedom early enough that the resultant energy of the bursting out was mostly put to constructive ends, in education and becoming teachers or givers of service in some way. Though rebellious, they were able to put their energies to much that Dan himself stood for. Joel, Phil, and Steve teach in universities; Larry is a medical doctor; and Jan explores ways of helping problem children.

The five are very close though separated by great distances. None of them now lives close to the place of their childhood. When they get together they look back on those days of simple and disciplined living with a great deal of nostalgia. The simple life is seen as both a source of humor and of a certain sense of pride.

The twins did not have winter coats until they were in seventh grade. They had just a few changes of clothing and some items which they would wear to the barn would be washed that night or the next morning and worn to church on Sunday. Why did they have several old cars, none of them in good working order? They agree now that their father's commitments to cutting back, to living on a small amount of money, refusing to accept increases in salary are very much in tune with a lot of good thinking today.

Their father's emphasis on being world citizens and getting to know people of differing cultures has made travelers of them all. BVS in Warsaw, Poland; the Peace Corps in Chile, South America; volunteer service in Cyprus; study in Lebanon, Taiwan, Germany, and Japan; plus much traveling in the United States, all these have been enjoyed by the children. Travel anywhere and everywhere is still exciting to them. And they would all agree with their father, "I have always found good people everywhere I've gone."

Dan's advice to keep one foot on the soil has been heeded by three of the children. The soil is close to the hearts of each of them. Gardening, fishing, watching birds, tramping in the sand, walking along the beach, hiking in the woods—it is in this environment that they feel a close kinship with their father.

Some of their father's ideas have remained with the children. None is a puritan or altruist in the way Dan was. Right and wrong exist for them, but they are not as rigid in their beliefs as their father. They see the human race as changing and evolving, but not as ever becoming perfect. They have a degree of conscience about the poor and unfortunate, and a couple of them suggest that some day the impact may be greater, but at this point their focus is not on the poor people in other lands nor in our own land.

All five feel they are more selfish than their father. They do not give "the last ounce of energy to help along some 'ugly duckling' as Dad did." Each of them enjoys life now, and that also means some of the comforts of life. Each likes to have a good time and will spend money, time, and effort to just that end alone, though all are frugal.

The recycling of everything has made them all savers—just in case. They see their father as a man ahead of his time in his advocacy of recycling, conservation of natural resources, and the care of one's body through exercise and correct nutrition. Though the conservation concern and the puritanical attitude toward the care of the body may not be as religious in emphasis as their father's, economically and realistically they agree that it makes sense.

As all of Dan's and Lucy's children have become successful and are tempted to be caught up into the consumer-oriented society, the nine grandchildren who are old enough to enjoy stories are attracted to reminiscences about simple life on the farm. As these are reenforced by ecological and environmental concerns which their parents heard about only at home, the grandchildren's lives may more nearly respond to the kind of ideal their grandfather had in mind.

The four West children who are teachers think of their father as a marvelous teacher from whom they can learn much. The way he related to large groups, small groups, and camping groups was unusual. He had a knack, a way of conveying a certain amount of support and at the same time challenging each person to pursue his or her own thoughts. That's an art that they still aspire to. He was a master at it, making each person in the group seem special to him. But the qualities that made him an excellent teacher were not necessarily the qualities that made him a good parent. Whereas they see him as a model as a teacher, they do not look upon him as a model for being a parent. A psychiatrist summed it up succinctly, "While I admire Dan I don't wish to be like him. . . . I think such literal idealism can hurt persons since it puts one's ideals ahead of the personal fulfillment of persons close by."

Selling off a portion of the farm to a neighbor and Steve's earning most of the money for his own ticket, enabled the three of them to take a trip around the world after Dan's retirement. On a tape made for Chauncey Shamberger at a reunion of Dan and Lucy West, Al and Mae Brightbill, and Perry and Ruth Rohrer in Chicago in 1960, Dan reported on the West's trip around the world. I'll let him tell you about it.

"Lucy, Steve and I took off by plane from New York City the middle of June, 1959, flew to Amsterdam, and then took a tour around in several countries for three weeks before we settled down to the work of the summer. Lucy went to a work camp in Bielefeld, Germany as co-director with senior refugees; Steve was in a work camp in Vienna, and I conducted a peace seminar in Kassel, Germany. We all had a good workout.

"After the Annual Conference of the Brethren in Europe, we stuck around a while and I visited my first, and only, heifer distribution in Germany. We took a VW the last of September and drove down through Switzerland, France, back to Spain where I was during their Civil War, then over to Italy. Going by train, plane, and ship we got to the Holy Land—about the most unholy place I've seen on this planet so far. I don't know the way out of the problem between the Arabs and the Israelis. I wish I could find someone who did see the answer to that problem because it is intolerable as it is.

"We spent some time in Egypt and northern Turkey, then flew from Ankara, to Teheran, then over to Bombay, India. I worked, all in all, in about fifteen countries on the Heifer Project. The idea seems essentially sound. We've done some good. I think there's a future for it if we've got what it takes to work it.

"Over in India I'm told the Brethren have been invited to join up with about a half dozen other churches there in forming the Church of Northern India. You see they have one church in Southern India and this would look reasonable. But I ran across something that bothers me a little—more than a little—it made me mad. It seems that the Brethren are welcome to join and wanted to join over there, if we accept infant baptism and the Apostolic Confession. Now here is where I got mad and haven't recovered from it yet. I think that if we cut out what our forefathers paid a good big price for originally, that we're not correctly their descendants. Certainly we don't dare to be as narrow as some of our people but it would be highly unfortunate if the Brethren flavor would get washed out in ecumenical movements, just as I think it would be highly unmoral if the Lutheran flavor would get washed out. I think I came back from our trip more of a Dunker than when I went. At the same time I'm more of a cooperator with other people, other Christians and non-Christians, if you please, but I don't think that's an easy thing any way you take it. In

Bangkok we found Christians, Jews and Muslims and Hindus and Buddhists. We liked them all, but we don't think we want to join their churches yet.

"We found good people everywhere we went and some of our friends and some Brethren. Saw one of the campers who was at Boone, Iowa in the 20s. He is the agricultural representative on a United States Overseas Mission at Bangkok. He was just as cordial as he ever was and grateful for the help that camp gave him. Glad we have people carrying the gospel in their own way. Wish we had more doing that.

"From Bangkok we flew to Hong Kong, then took a ship. Couldn't get permission to go into China and it might not have been the healthiest for everyone if we had gone. However, I do not think we can continue to insist that China does not exist. What to do next is not clear, but I think we have not recognized them officially sometimes. I'd like to see the Heifer Project put some cattle in there and help them otherwise. I think the common people are to be trusted under everybody's government, and I think we had better make friends with those people or otherwise we'll kill each other off.

"We then went to Japan by boat from Hong Kong. Spent three weeks in Japan, and it was very meaningful and very interesting. I kinda hated to come home but we wanted to get the garden out. We left Yokohoma on March 16, and arrived at San Francisco on March 28."

Dan then handed the microphone over to Lucy, who continued: "Dan was up to the same things he used to be. Way back in October, 1959, Dan and the twins made up that they would meet us in San Francisco. Steve and I didn't know anything about it, so when we came into dock on that old ship, Dan was on the deck with his field glasses. I said, 'There's no point, Dan, in being out here; there'll be no one to see us.' But down below there were two tall guys whom we were terribly happy to see. It had been so long, especially with Phil, who had been in Japan, that I didn't recognize them. But you can be sure we were mighty happy to see them."

Dan's charisma was evident wherever they went. The whole trip was full of people and places, not just people one meets as a tourist, but farmer and peasant types who genuinely appreciated the help of the Heifer Project International. They traveled something like 43,000 miles in about thirty countries in ten months.

In a letter Dan wrote to a friend, he reported, "It was a good trip we three took around the world, but like a cow out on heavy pasture I need some time to chew my cud and digest it. That is happening, and it brings new meaning to some events on the trip. But it makes me both grateful and critical of what we have and have not done in the USA. My job now is to keep my home base on our farm (and do a little work to keep fit) but also to reach out to a world in the making."

15
Credo

That Dan was a thinker, an idealist, and a philosopher no one doubted. Letters to friends were not the usual "How are you? I am fine" or "We did this; we did that," though he always acknowledged with gratitude any letter to him, "It was good to hear from you," and the characteristic closing, "Truly—Dan." Just as when he talked with people, his letters were not idle chatter nor even "keeping in touch" kinds of things. Some time during the conversation or in the letter, Dan interjected a question to consider, a quotation to ponder, or a book to read.

William James perhaps influenced Dan's thinking as much as any one person. *The Will to Believe* suggested that what a person gives credence to has important psychological consequences in his life, is capable of making him either a "sick-soul" or a "healthy-minded" man, and therefore everyone has the right to choose those beliefs that will keep him healthy, happy, and at home in the world in which he must live. Dan had made that choice.

A book which Dan often suggested to his friends was *Rational Living* (1905) by Henry Churchill King. It had meant much to him in a period of uncertainty when he was testing ideas and beliefs. It did not seem to strike fire with one of his correspondents, so Dan countered with another suggestion, Annie Payson Call's *The Freedom of Life* (1905). Perhaps the book which influenced Dan's personality most was *Happiness* by Karl Hilty. Dan valued this book partially for the quotation, "The sons of this age are shrewder in their relation to their own age than the sons of light." Dan deeply believed the next generation would improve upon the previous one. He didn't give up completely on the world even when he was physically weak and unable to talk. In a letter written only six months before his death his last sentence was: "For Jesus' sake—and the world as it is becoming."

Dan noted in a letter to another friend, "Once I was miserable when I noted how far I had missed happiness; then I ceased to care much about that, and tried to make others happier; since then I am much happier myself." This philosophy was expressed in a poem Dan often repeated:

> *I sought my soul,*
> *But my soul could not see.*
> *I sought my God,*
> *But my God eluded me.*
> *I sought my brother*
> *And found all three.*
> (Author unknown)

Dan had complete faith in truth and in the belief that truth would make one free. Because he believed each person was "in process," always growing, always discovering new truths, he gave this advice:

    a. Don't be discouraged or ashamed of what you believe to be true at a given time.

    b. Think it through, prepare it, write it down, sign it, date it, and then leave it on the shelf.

Then he would add, "Though you may not have it 'all together' at that time, someone else may later pick it up and use it as a germ to get him started to thinking." Dan believed in sharing his beliefs, the truth as he saw it at that time. And he followed his advice about dating his thoughts.

Joe Van Dyke, a philosopher himself who enjoyed discussions with Dan, via mail, received a letter from Dan with an enclosure entitled a "Cross-section of What I Believe" (dated, spring 1928):

"1. I believe in laws (probably sequences): physical, chemical, biological, psychological, spiritual. I cannot draw sharp lines between those fields, however; Drummond says the same laws operate in the natural and spiritual worlds. He is helpful to me *(The Natural Law in the Spiritual World)*.

"2. I believe in after-thots (sic). History is a part of them. Shailer Matthews says we get the idea of the direction of a ship's course from the wake in the water; so with the idea of human progress—we infer it from the "wake" of history.

"3. I believe in intelligence: the placing of worthy goals, the adapting of means to reach them, and self-criticism. I believe that the best ways of living can endure the light of rational criticism.

"4. I believe in goodness, the kind of action and attitude that abides, that can be built upon. 'The bad man annuls today what he did yesterday. The good man builds today upon what he did yesterday.'—W. T. Harris.

"5. I believe in friendship, the integrating of spirit of several persons, to their mututal helpfulness and lasting happiness.

"6. I believe in sacrifice as investment and net gain, not net loss—water on higher levels because it was not allowed to leak in the basement.

"7. I believe in evolution as the process God is still using in guiding the universe, and the process used by good men and women, the process at work in all religions, and culminating in the life of the Master. The goal of evolution is Jesus Christ.— H. Drummond. Donald Hankey's *Religion and Common Sense* is good. As to evolution of one's own faith, there is a good phrase from Tennyson—faith that comes of self-control.

"8. I believe that the Power back of the universe is not aimless, not self-destructive, not opposed to personal values, but going somewhere, 'kind in His justice,' and at least as much as personal, perhaps much more. It is a great synthesis in one word—God. Only Judaism and Christianity have made that great generalization.

"9. I believe in the 'more abundant life' to give which to other people was the big drive back of the Master's life—a cyclical integration of the most honest thot (sic), and the widest knowledge, and the best choices in living into a continually increasing happiness and helpfulness—so that any time we may pause to look up from work, and think a bit, we can strike a balance, and say sincerely that life is good, and that it promises even greater good. I don't need to say that I *believe* this—I know it."

Almost every time Dan set down in rather precise terms what he thought or believed, he would begin or end with some similar qualification: "Here is the outline (incomplete) of my best interpretation now. In a few more years it ought to be better and fuller."

A bit of philosophy was often tacked to the bottom of a letter in the form of a P.S.—one, dated 4/29/28: "Regarding morality, unmorality, and immortality these: I believe there can be no unmorality where there is intelligence. We are immoral when we know the good and don't act so, or when we know a course of action is wrong but still follow it. 'He that knoweth to do good and doeth it not, to him it is sin.' For that we do not need sympathy, I opine, but the lash of public opinion to stir our sluggish or ineffective consciences. D. W."

A note written by Dan on an envelope addressed to Mr. and Mrs. Dan West, postmarked January 27, 1961, expressed his continuous search for truth, including doubt at times, even after retirement: "Sometimes I wonder if I am out of it for clinging to such things as hope, faith, and love. Camus in *The Stranger* (1946) would say that I am. But my life is too much grounded in facts of love. This I know. Deep as these doubts are that Camus helps me to see within me, my present direction—is faith!"

A few years before Dan's death, Joe Van Dyke started a round robin letter with Dan, Chauncey Shamberger, Al Brightbill, and Perry Rohrer. In one of his last letters Dan enclosed a list of things he was dreaming about—some ideas which were ruminating in a mind that was still active and still raising long range questions at the age of 76. He called them "Prunes, which still need a little soaking."

Some General Prunes:
Are ALL men created equal?

Shall we be rooted in history?
How shall we turn to the changing world?
Morality appropriate to this world and God
Openness—what kind and how much?
Some good four-letter words: Work, love, hope, wait, etc.

Some Personal Prunes:
What kind of mixture are you?
What are your impulses, selves, and GOALS?
What do you think about?
Your impulses and your "selves"?
You are "hungry for what"?
Looking in the rear view mirror?
How much fun do you have to have?
Do you love your neighbor as yourself?

If we love our neighbors as ourselves, as Jesus commanded, Dan then asked, "Can We Feed This Hungry World?"
(The Christian Century, Jan. 18, 1950). After a discussion of
the surpluses existing in various parts of the world at that
time, organizations which were attempting to deal with the
problem of distribution, and the responsibility individual
citizens must face, Dan continued:

"This business of getting food to the world's hungry is *our*
job, and I am confident it can be done. Also I am sure of the
direction in which to work, of a few steps to take now, and of
the motive which should control what we do. Fundamentally, it
is a religious problem as much as one in economics.

"1. If *we love our neighbors as ourselves,* we will set as
one of our main goals feeding the hungry world as much, as
well, and as soon as we can. That includes those we call communists, in spite of what they think and do and want.

"2. Again, *if we love our neighbors as ourselves,* we will
determine to produce more food and to move our surplus as
fast as it accumulates, whether we make money on the transac-
tion or not. . . .

"3. Also, *if we love our neighbors as ourselves,* we will
spread these dollars around, through investment in foreign
agriculture and industries, so that the little people can have

seeds and tools and know-how. . . .

"4. Further, *if we love our neighbors as ourselves*, we shall stretch our loyalties until we belong more to the world than to our own nation. A man without a country is in bad shape, but a man whose loyalty is frozen at national boundaries is out of date *now*. . . .

"5. If *we love our neighbors as ourselves*, we will put a ceiling on our wants, ration ourselves down to the point of physical efficiency—and then share with the hungry majority. . . .

"6. Finally, *if we love our neighbors as ourselves*, we will not stop with being critical at inappropriate policy or action on the surplus problem. . . .

"We North Americans are for the time being living in the most favored place in the world. . . . We *can* move the hungry world—toward peace!"

16
To Speak the Truth in Love

Searching for answers Dan constantly sought the counsel of authorities in various fields. The depression, banks closing, and unsettled economic conditions concerned Dan. Bringing together economists—a Quaker and a Mennonite—Dan asked penetrating questions about the American system of economics, socialism and its effect in Germany, and the interrelatedness of war and economic conditions.

On sabbatical in 1954, Dan spent a large portion of his time browsing around in three universities—Harvard, Michigan, and Chicago. After being away from the university for more than thirty years, it seemed good to get back and swap notes. He was delighted with what he found in the way of new discoveries, especially new research, and, of course, the new findings in human relations were exciting to him.

In a letter written during this time, he shared these thoughts, "Nine years ago Archibald MacLeish said, 'We now accept the miracle of the atom, but we do not yet accept the miracle of the heart.' That fascinates me. I talked with him about it at Harvard and I am on the search of every effort that I can discover in that direction. Some day we will learn how and once we have what it takes to do it, we will start and maintain the chain reaction of the spirit. Don't ask me what all that means, but I want to learn within the next ten years."

Before his retirement in 1959, Dan wanted to pull together the ideas he had found to be successful and rewarding to him in the discussion approach with young people in Sunday school classes, camp forums, and church councils. A booklet, *Thinking Together,* which he wrote in 1948, was a start in this direction.

Inviting two college professors who had worked with him in human relations labs, in CPS programs during World War II, and in various church-related activities, Dan suggested that they hitchhike on each others' ideas and write a book on communicative skills.

The pattern was to determine goals, develop an outline, and assign responsibilities for the writing. They exchanged their creative efforts through the mail and got together periodically to destroy or extend what they had been doing. Though Dan made contacts with at least two publishers neither saw the manuscript as a safe gamble. The project spanned five to seven years, terminating in 1956, but the effort was not in vain for working together helped each of them to clarify his own thinking.

The work sessions were a good example of shared leadership. Dan was the prime mover, but all took responsibility for seeing that things moved along. Though Dan may have had subtle ways of encouraging a group to move in the direction that he wanted them to move, in these work sessions he proved authentically flexible. There may have been times when he gave up a point of view reluctantly or when he really hoped to convince the other two of the error of their ways eventually, but once they had decided on a direction he pitched in to develop it whether it had been his idea or not.

As late as September, 1969, the collaboration of Dan with two men, also proponents of the simple life, resulted in a long article in *Messenger.* In it they suggested that "where money and other things are used as necessary tools in right living, in loving God and world neighbors as yourselves, the Christian ideal is approached. The Christian use of money should start from this attitude." But they went on to say that television, newspapers, magazines, radio, and direct mail all offer us many things we do not really need. The feeling that "we must keep up with the Joneses" does real damage to many good people. Putting a ceiling on wants, avoiding the waste of time and money, and refraining from postponing payments through use of credit cards were some valid principles to follow. "If *wants* are simple, there may be more *time* available for God's work."

"Good Dunkards," Dan often said, "have had a self-rationing program for centuries. They called it the simple life."

But on some Sunday mornings the "simple life" made for a most complicated life in the West family. The cars on the farm, all together worth less than a thousand dollars, were hard to start if it was cold or wet. The boys had to get a horse hitched up to start the tractor, to pull the car up the hill so they could all get to Sunday school by 9:30. The simple life would have been simpler with two newer, workable cars. But the boys were accustomed to doing this, so they accepted it as something they had to do, and it did not seem to be out of the ordinary to them at that time.

Early contacts with Dan left the impression that he lived frugally, acquiring little property, sharing his family's wealth, living directly off the soil, and living the simple life. Some of his friends were surprised, however, to find that his home was quite well furnished and that his family enjoyed most of the usual comforts of life. While Dan did eat frugally (except at friends' homes) and dressed unimpressively, he traveled extensively. While this was primarily for vocational reasons, he thoroughly enjoyed the exhilaration of hobnobbing with those who were less conspicious in their consumption. He reveled in rubbing shoulders with individuals of the governmental and academic arenas. He loved good literature and good music. In these areas he was less frugal. In fact, frugality in some areas left more monies available for those experiences which he ranked high in importance.

Conspicuous spending on the part of others often received Dan's comments. His terse remark, "You're getting into a lot of expense here," followed by an admonition about the wise use of money, seemed a bit frank to a 38-year-old doctor who had established his practice and was remodeling a farmhouse for his family.

Dan, in some correspondence with a Mennonite author, wrote his thoughts on simple living:

"My conviction is that simplicity is related essentially to integrity, that the simple life is the integrated life with all of the essentials included, with all marginal values, 'accessories,' excluded. From this point of view, simplicity is possible on many levels and in many varied situations. There is the simple faith of persons who take the New Testament too literally, not knowing the background. There's another simple faith achieved by great scholars who round the circle of learning with a humble heart. Someone observed that 'perfect ignorance is calm. Perfect knowledge is calm. In between is the storm.' That is directly related to the idea of simplicity."

That Dan had many topics of discussion was assumed. Usually his techniques did not startle anyone, but once in the 60s at Elizabethtown, Pennsylvania his proposal seemed a bit out-of-the-ordinary. Upon his arrival at the church Dan suggested that he needed something to make his presentation more visual and graphic. He wanted a ladder! The pastor cringed at the prospect of an ugly, paint-splattered ladder "gracing" the lovely new sanctuary which had recently been dedicated. But the pastor followed through on Dan's request and placed the ladder on the new red carpet of the chancel. An embarrassed janitor, thinking someone had inadvertently left the ladder after replacing a light bulb, relegated it to the basement again. At Dan's insistence the ladder was returned and again placed on the chancel. The organist, thinking, "It couldn't be!"struggled to get it into one of the back rooms before the parishioners began arriving. By now the pastor was exasperated. He retrieved the vanishing ladder, remained in the sanctuary to keep an eye on it, and to await the reactions of the unsuspecting congregation on seeing an old ladder in their new church!

Once the meeting started, however, no one noticed the inappropriate paint-splattered prop which Dan had chosen to illustrate his message. As was his genius, he got the group involved even while he was making the presentation on "The Levels of Fellowship." Using a card on which he had printed the activity related to each level, Dan hung the card on a rung of the ladder as he dealt with each aspect of fellowship.

The first level was *Eating Together*. That needed little explanation for eating has always been associated with fellowship. He placed the card, *Eating Together,* on the first rung. The second level was *Playing Together*. Dramatically he strolled over to the ladder and placed *Playing Together* on the next rung. Level three, he explained, was *Working Together*. He was very convincing at this point, for Dan had long been an exponent of big muscle work; helping a neighbor was a high level of fellowship, whether it was helping to build a barn or planting a field. *Working Together* was added to the ladder.

Thinking Together was point number four. This was being demonstrated as Dan's listeners were beginning to think with Dan. Then came *Serving Together*. No problem. Service has been the middle name for the Brethren. This was no surprise to the group; Brethren had helped in service projects— clothing, heifers, refugee resettlement—sharing with those less fortunate was part of their living. So *Serving Together* was added to the ladder.

But what would level six be? they wondered. Next, explained Dan, was *Worshiping Together*. Why hadn't they thought of that! Of course, worship produced that feeling of oneness, togetherness, of closeness to each other. In an inspirational message Dan suggested the merits of Christians coming together to praise God and to affirm each other. Heads were nodding in approval. He hung *Worshiping Together* in its place. Then Dan, after well-timed moments of silence for contemplative thinking, pulled out his trump card. The highest level, and here Dan paused again (another level? the congregation wondered)—the highest level was *Suffering Together*. That was the most meaningful level of fellowship. *Suffering Together* was placed on the top level of the ladder. The old, decrepit, paint-splattered ladder had served its purpose; Dan had clearly made his point.

One day in September, 1937, just before he crossed the French frontier into Franco Spain, Dan had a dream, a dream he continued to espouse. His dream was of *The Coming Brotherhood,* the title of a 96-page booklet he published in

1938. In the preface Dan states: "The kingdom of God is much larger than the Church of the Brethren. But we can make a valuable contribution . . . if we fill to overflowing the doctrines of brotherhood which we have claimed, and, in part, manifested for two hundred and thirty years.

"There is only one way for people to live if they want to be brethren. It is the way Jesus lived and taught . . . we shall have to choose between this way of living and the destruction . . . of civilization. Whatever we American Christians do . . . some day people will live on this earth as brethren, following the commandments that Jesus gave. . . . If we strive at our best, that might happen within the next fifty years in America, where we have a better chance than elsewhere."

Dan detailed four ways people can help each other:

(a) Mutual aid—the direct approach which would use "big muscles." Dan often said, "Love is the Lord's Prayer in overalls."

(b) Credit unions which would make available "the security of the whole brotherhood to every responsible brother." Because of Dan's urgings the Common Bond Credit Union, Inc. was organized in the state of Ohio on January 13, 1937. Membership was and is open to members of the Church of the Brethren in Southern Ohio. Originally one unit, which cost five dollars, was difficult to get and amounts as low as twenty-five cents were accepted for credit in the members' books in those early days. The large amount of money in that credit union today, the interest aspect, and the connection with Ohio laws would boggle Dan's mind.

(c) The student loan fund, under the church's administration, had Dan's approval, but he questioned using National Youth Administration funds from the government for educating youth.

(d) Life insurance and old age support for the church's missionaries and ministers was all right, but Dan didn't want it to stop there. Every helpless brother—minister, missionary, or layman and his dependents—should be cared for "just because we are brethren."

About sex, Dan wrote that the old tradition that sex was evil but necessary has been changed by the acceptance of it as a natural fact. But, he said, the attitude of most modern Americans, older and younger, would hardly fit with the New Testament. The recent reaction against prudery in the name of self-expression and the former prudery itself have this in common—both overemphasize sex. Sex, he continued, is an instinct and we are responsible for its use and control. There is no truth in the contention that satisfaction is healthy and continuence unhealthy. "It is the task of the church to build, in the parents first, the attitude of wholesome acceptance of the implications of sex, and, at the same time, the habit of control for Christian purposes much as we have learned to control electricity for further purposes."

Dan was hard on the romantic inclinations of youth. The ideal male-female relations among youth was sublimation, according to Dan. Only thus could one maintain the respect of personality. "The delicate bloom of the grape will not stand much handling," he said and then pointed out that he was not referring to the blossom, but to the dust-like surface on ripe grapes that shows up best when they are cool and moist. He would be shocked, confused, and even hostile about the loose sex patterns of many youth and adults today.

In Dan's dream of the "brotherhood that will come some day," the most commonly used materials will include the direct experiences of the people in that brotherhood. "It will center largely about the activities of keeping fit, making friends, making a living, building homes, raising children, getting along with many people, understanding the big world, trying to find meanings back of birth, growth, and death, and groping for the meaning of the long future. It will certainly include the great crises that come to members as persons and in groups."

To the question, How will we get all of these specialists to carry out the plan for The Coming Brotherhood? Dan gave the answer, "Find them where they are not discovered. Give them jobs. Then raise the rest of them. We have a lot of likely 'cubs' "—referring to his famous phrase, "If you want bear stew, first get the bear."

"Another Man's Opinion" was written by a friend who had had many discussions with Dan on some of these subjects. A few quotations will show their differences: "Let's be done with this hypocrisy of accepting the protection and benefits of the sovereign state in peacetime and turning anarchist in war-times. A profound distruct of the state in time of war has been transferred to a distrust in peacetime state action as well. By inference the state is conceived as an evil to be replaced by the church." And, "The church, as West sees it, is to become a sanctified home demonstration agent guiding the thinking on home life, recreation, leisure time, right use of money, proper budgeting, and other personal and social problems. . . . Regarding credit unions or mutual life insurance—if the cooperative action remains small it will not affect the national economy enough to build a peaceful world. If the church-controlled cooperative gets large, it too will soon be controlled by a small inside group at the top. . . . The Brethren should consider carefully the power of the modern state and government for potential good as well as evil, with the church helping to guide the action of the state rather than building a church economic system."

On June 21, 1938, one of Dan's greatest admirers wrote "An Open Letter to Dan West." Dan's influence on his life in many areas was noted with great appreciation. "You guided my reading for several years. Present or absent, you have stimulated and colored my thinking. . . . Any people, all people, mean more to me for my having known you. As I write, my feelings in the presence of a June sunset are richer for my having taken part in several vesper services led by you. . . .

"Though I doubt if you taught me to doubt, you at least removed my doubts as to the unmixed evil of doubt . . . and supplementary to and more useful than the encouragement of honest doubt was the stress you placed upon the making of equally honest effort to seek behind or beyond the point in doubt. . . .

"Lately I have begun to recognize what I believe is a serious weakness in your system. It is, I am sure, one of technique, and not of intent. . . . It is your failure to wean your disciples soon enough. Perhaps the weakness lies in us. . . . It shows in the difficulty which so many of us have in developing our own thought-patterns, and substituting them for the ready-mades with which you supplied us. Brilliant and admirable though your philosophy and teachings were, we have failed too long to realize that they were *yours,* that few people—probably no other person—can find it possible to adapt to the world as it is in just the way you do. You hammered and forged your philosophy in the agonizing smithy of your own experience; you 'earned your right to speak'; we tried to take short-cuts. . . . Hand-me-downs simply don't fit. . . .

"I venture to assert that you have developed fewer variants than halting imitators, more pale carbons of yourself and your ideas than independent thinkers and advocates. . . . I question in my own mind whether you really expected us to accept your teachings, and adapt your pattern of life, so literally. . . . On the other hand, may there not be the possibility that in your gropings, both for policies to teach, and for methods of presenting them, you sometimes have been a bit over-eager and over-zealous—that you have over-awed some of us by the brilliance of your advocacies—that you have given us visions without helping us to anticipate intervening difficulties. . . . Might your teaching not become still more effective if you were to place more emphasis on the right of, and the need for, individuals to vary from the trails you lay, and blaze others for themselves?

"To speak the truth in love—what a task and what a risk! But I remember that one of your favorite quotations is the first clause of First Corinthians 13:4 (Love is patient and kind)."

Writing in 1947, Dan suggested that "in the last third of a century we [the Church of the Brethren] have moved so far and so fast that were my own father to return he would not likely recognize the same church to which he belonged." Dan quoted one observer, outside the Church of the Brethren, "The Brethren are moving faster than any other church in America."

Most of these changes, Dan believed, had demonstrated the genius of the Brethren in action. To support this contention Dan cited such developments as the Brethren support of the American Friends Service Committee in the Spanish Civil War relief, when the Brethren were the only group with workers on both sides; the heifer project, in which Catholic and Lutheran workers cooperated (and now we can add CROP,

Christian Rural Overseas Program, which was just being started when Dan wrote the article); the UNRRA program which
was modified by the Brethren ideas and cooperation; the
Church World Service program, which "might not have happened without the Brethren."

Dan concluded that the future was "uncertain as yet but
potentially far beyond anything in our history." According to
him the question was, and still is, whether the Brethren would
continue to develop their social policy as rapidly as they had
done in the past fifty years, or whether they had reached the
point where an inevitable leveling-off would take place.

Perhaps Dan would say today, as he wrote in the family's
Christmas newsletter in 1944: "God is still in his heaven . . .
and here on earth too trying to help us floundering mortals to
learn how we ought to live in homes, in churches, in communities, and in the world. *He shouldn't have to wait so long
on us!*"

17

The Hard Work
of Letting Go

In 1965, at the age of 72, Dan was chosen moderator-elect of the Church of the Brethren Annual Conference. That was a year of preparation for the next year when he would become the moderator. This task necessitated much travel (Lucy took a year's leave to travel with him) and a heavy leadership role.

Then in 1966, holding high a towel as a symbol of order, service, patience, and love for one another, Dan West, first lay moderator, opened the business session of the 180th recorded Annual Conference of the Church of the Brethren at Louisville, Kentucky. This gesture was no surprise, for Dan was loved and known throughout the brotherhood as peacemaker, a relief worker and a good discussion leader. A towel represented Dan's way of working with people more appropriately than did a gavel. But before the conference had ended the authority of the gavel and Robert's *Rules of Order* had often been invoked. Though he attempted desperately hard to be fair and to allow everyone who wished to speak, as he had done in working with small groups, Dan's methods created some disorder among the 1,183 delegate voting members.

Confusion was the word Dan used in his keynote address the evening before to characterize the state of the denomination. The word was also aptly applied to the first business ses-

sion with the moderator himself tallying up his own "slips" as
the debate—to continue as observers or to become participants
in the Consultation on Church Union—grew in intensity. During the entire week, persons behind the scenes had to tie loose
ends left dangling by Dan's unorthodox way of handling the
conference. From the very beginning when, at Dan's insistence, the flag hanging inconspicuously at the rear of the
auditorium was removed, through the parliamentary jostling
which elicited his oft repeated reminder that one minute
wasted was the equivalent of twenty hours of delegates' time,
to the passing of the gavel, one could sense that Dan, though
still active and alert, did not always have the energy nor the
flexibility which the task demanded.

    Although many conferees may have gone home wonder-
ing whether the Brethren were confused or still open to the
searching for new opportunities in which to be faithful servants, the moderator's address was positive in its affirmation
that resources were available which would give direction and
stability to the denomination. One resource, he said, was
Brethren heritage. "I'm not favoring ancestor worship, just
honest bookkeeping. If we fulfill the best from our home
culture we can look our children in the eye and urge them to
do better than we. They can urge their children to improve on
that."

    The Bible was another available resource, he emphasized.
"We Christians have spent more time worshiping the signpost
than following the road. For me, the New Testament is a
gambler's handbook giving rules for betting our lives that Jesus
is the way, the truth, and the life."

    The record of accomplishments through the years should
give guidance and hope. Foreign missions and those activities
with which he had been so closely involved—work camps, conscientious objectors, Brethren Volunteer Service, and the
Heifer Project—were listed. But as Dan had said so often, the
greatest resource was the people within the church. He
emphasized the potential among the laity. He had challenged
persons time and time again in small groups, such as Hilltops,
peace seminars, human relations labs and Mission 12 retreats,
with the words, "You folks right here can change the world!"

Though he described the church in 1966 as "more confused than I have ever seen it before" and warned that "we
may be headed for greater confusion," he, an optimist, affirmed that it need not be so, but it will take love, openness,
thinking, courage, prayer, work and commitment to Jesus
Christ as Lord and to the servant role he exemplified.

Toward the end of the 60s it was apparent that Dan's
health was failing. His low energy and his increasing age
began to show on him. They were starting to show up before
he was willing to step back and let other leaders assume the
heavier leadership roles. Probably he was ailing even before
the disease was identified, but he did not seem to see the ap-
propriateness of stepping back from a leading position in the
church quite soon enough. His reticence to leave the role made
it rough for him as well as for other people. He surely was
aware of the fact that he did not have the persuasive ability
that he had had, he did not have quite the flexibility in terms
of thinking on his feet that he had before, and he did not
always have the command of respect of the people he was
working with. At this point Dan did not recognize the necessi
ty of his letting go of leadership; or he may have recognized it
but wanted to deny it.

There may be another related factor. Dan never had what
would be called avocational interests that could consume his
time, his interests, and his dollars. His vocational interests may
have driven him to hang onto his role as leader. He could, and
would, talk about other kinds of activities—manual tasks and
hobbies—but had little enthusiasm for them. This was
reflected in the kinds of things he saved. He saved a number of
post cards—not many; he saved a variety of coins, but again
not many. He took an interest in plants, and yet he did not
really work at caring for them. He did not really anticipate the
consequences of growing older, and he did not entertain the
idea of shifting gears vocationally.

In 1966 Steve West went to Cyprus as a volunteer. The
decision was his own, for he had a genuine interest in the Middle East by this time. Being free of his earlier reaction to his
father, Steve invited his parents to visit in the summer of his
second year there, 1967. By now it was a good feeling for Steve

to have his father there without any anxiety about how he would react to their differences. For the first time Dan's youngest son was able to be himself and let his father relate to him however he wanted to.

It was a disappointment to find that Dan's health was not up to par. Dan came as a leader of discussions as he had always done. Only this time the people there (mostly from Europe, and about 40 of them) were not Brethren. They smoked and drank and were far more liberal in their behavior than Brethren youth of earlier decades. This bothered Dan deeply. In one session he refused to go ahead with the program unless they stopped smoking. For Steve this no longer made him angry at his father; rather, he felt sorry for him. It was sad because the old pattern of puritanism prevented Dan from moving ahead with these alert and bright youth on some issues of substance. That was a difficult time for Dan. Never before had he been in such heat, and that with poor health really wilted him.

Steve later received an International Distinguished Service Award from Macalester College for his work in Cyprus. Dan evidenced real pride. It was satisfying for him to know that his son really enjoyed his work there, a work that his dad fully supported.

In 1960, Dan wrote to a friend who was ill: "Puny as a child and delicate in youth, I have had abundant reason for gratitude for good health I have enjoyed most of my life. And I feel keenly for anybody who is ill. Last winter in India I knew what weakness is on a long stretch—about six weeks. But so far as I know I am back to normal again and am very grateful.

"We do not know yet why [there are] some kinds of illnesses, and we are only beginning to learn what possibilities there are for rising above the illnesses using the setbacks in life for spiritual gain. Maybe you can be helpful here." Dan would be needing that help in a few years.

When the children came home for the holidays in 1966-68 their mother would express, in whispers, her concern that their father did not seem to be himself; he seemed extra tired, not really healthy and well. On his own, and alone, Dan went to the Cleveland Clinic just before Christmas 1968 for three days of medical examination. The diagnosis: amytrophic lateral sclerosis (Lou Gehrig's Disease, ALS); the prognosis: progressive suffering and gradual paralysis, sure death.

Because Dan did not discuss his health problem, it was difficult for those around him and dear to him. He simply told them he had the disease and let them draw their own conclusions. Larry, in internship, explained to his brothers and sister that one of the characteristics of persons with the disease was not to talk about it because they didn't recognize it as a disease. It was extremely hard for anyone to comfort Dan. He did not ask for comfort and seemed not to recognize it when members of the family wanted to give it. As Jan expressed it, "I think comfort is not just for the person receiving it. It's like giving gifts; the giver wants and needs to give. I feel the same way about someone who is sick and dying."

Though the student doctor tried to help his father realize the futility of trying to overcome death and the suffering that would ensue, Dan simply was not able to accept that diagnosis and prognosis. He continued to be cheerful and hopeful that something would change, feeling that all the discipline of eating right and keeping himself fit with daily walking and exercise should, and would, pay off.

It was true that he had kept a youthful spirit all through his life and in his own way kept on growing but the certainty of the disease and death aged him tremendously, and he did not become adaptable. When his voice began to fail his son urged him to take up crafts, for his hands were still normal; but Dan was an idea man, and he kept writing many, many notes for his mind remained clear to the end.

On Saturday, July 12, 1969, the 25th anniversary of the Heifer Project, honor was given to the founder of the program, Dan West. More than 1,500 persons gathered at Goshen, Indiana, the birthplace of Heifer Project.

In showing appreciation for the past, Thurl Metzger executive secretary of HPI for 17 years, presented Dan with an engraved, giant-sized, solid-brass Swiss cowbell, cast in Switzerland, a symbol of the significant work Dan had started and for his service in the church through the years.

Philip presented his father's acceptance speech. Though

Dan was present, he was unable to speak to the assembly, by then having experienced an almost total loss of speech.

As a symbolic gift, two beautiful young steers, a Jersey and a Holstein, were given to B. D. Kumar, a representative of the Embassy of India. The two purebred animals were to be included in the November shipment of half of the promised 180 animals.

Vance Hartke, US Senator from Indiana, the guest speaker, expressed appreciation for the work of the organization in the past but urged, "The Heifer Project type of work must be multiplied. Use your voices and your lives to do more and more to turn the world away from war and direct it toward peace."

It was a significant occasion, marking a dream of twenty-five years ago which expanded beyond the wildest imagination of the creative man who had the vision. "Dan West's heifer will go right on poking its warm nose over the world's fences," suggested one participant.

Paying tribute to the leadership of Dan West, the Middlebury (Indiana) Church of the Brethren held a recognition service on Sunday, August 24, 1969. Former associates and friends were invited to attend and/or write letters to be placed in a book and given to Dan at the time of the celebration.

The many, many letters received recounted the great numbers of activities in which Dan was involved, related the influence of his life on theirs, and recalled events experienced together. One letter written by his pastor added an observation not often mentioned, " . . . while you made me uncomfortable at times when I would visit you, by your time consciousness, you have helped me gain a new perspective on the value of time and the need for the wise use of it. . . . "

In conclusion he wrote, "As we pay tribute to you, Dan, for your significant leadership over the years, we would be remiss if we did not give recognition to Lucy and the part she has played in supporting, motivating, and encouraging you in your work, in addition to the outstanding leadership which she has given. . . . Well done thou good and faithful servants, enter into the joy of thy Lord."

From colleagues who worked closely with Dan came these words—Ralph Smeltzer: "Dan, you have been a *tall* man in many ways . . . You stood very tall in the eyes of youth . . . you stood tall in the eyes of all of us interested in peace . . . you stool taller than anyone else in the Brethren work-camp movement . . . Perhaps, Dan, you stood tallest in our eyes when you combined the ideal of peace with the practice of relief in the Heifer Project. We said you 'got Christianity down where you could milk it' . . . Dan, you've always stood tall—with tall ideas, tall dedication, tall inspiration, tall friendship. I only pray that those of us who may carry on your concerns can match to some degree your tallness. I know that my 33 years' association with you has made me a lot taller."

W. Harold Row: "Your life in the church and in the world community has been both distinguished and distinctive. Few if any have given more dedicated and perceptive leadership in the long history of our church. In this connection one thinks of your pioneer role in summer camps, youth programs, work camps, volunteer service, heifer project, peace education and action, leadership development, and functional democracy. In all of these you more than anyone else in our brotherhood have provided the ideological base and first practical demonstrations on which others have established programs. In a genuine sense, Dan, you have been our architect of brotherhood. . . . "

Four of the children, Steve, Joel, Jan and Phil were able to attend the recognition service. Al Brightbill was the guest music leader for the service. A tribute, "The Measure of a Man," not only honored Dan but recognized the contribution of his wife, Lucy, who was presented a bouquet of a dozen roses, a complete surprise to her.

Since Dan was unable to speak, Phil again spoke the appreciation of the family. A message on the bulletin for that service read: "To all who came to know him, whatever their beliefs or practices, the lanky, white-haired Hoosier is a kindly but incisive prophet, probing quietly but poignantly at the conscience of the church and of the future."

18
Markings on
the Graph

Because of the increasing paralysis of his throat and voice, it was predicted that Dan would die by choking on his food. The children made the decision on February 2, 1970, to have a gastrostomy performed so nutrition could be poured directly into the stomach through a tube. Caring for Dan became increasingly difficult for Lucy, and because, as the children said, "We don't want two tragedies," Dan was taken from the hospital to a nursing home in Elkhart (Indiana). The family felt some sense of guilt because of their inability to care for Dan and because they sensed his agony of isolation from them. He seemed unable to form close and open relationships with other people, and so was very lonely.

But Dan enjoyed a good discussion, even as late as the summer of 1970, when he could no longer speak and was very weak. Writing notes to two of the sons who had come for a visit, Dan was giving his views on society as it related to the way they raised their children. The suggestions about the kinds of values they should instill in their offspring were strong and definite. It was the same old story; they had heard it a thousand times. Finally, unable to keep still any longer, one son told Dan that he appreciated his concern for the grandchildren, he would listen to what he had to say, but ultimately the responsibility for training the children was theirs. Dan was not upset; perhaps he was even a bit happy to see how strongly his son responded, for Dan always enjoyed a "good scrap" intellectually. Between Christmas and New Years (1970) part of the family came home for the holidays. Dan was sufficiently alert to communicate with them by hand, to smile, and to write some notes, though he was in bed most of the time.

Larry, the medical doctor, tells the story of his father's last few days often, for to him it demonstrates the strength of character and perhaps the final admission and acceptance by his father of his own death. "After we left (following the holidays) he must have decided to die. On January 4, in sub-zero weather with a howling cold snowstorm outside, Dad went out in his pajamas, an overcoat, and his boots and began taking walks in the evening, though it was dark. We had talked with the nurses long before to let him call his own shots so they allowed him to walk out. He came back in, choking and coughing, but instead of going to his room, he sat on the couch in the lobby, warmed up a bit, went out for a second trip. Again, he came back in, warmed up a bit, and went for a third trip in the cold night air. I had walked with Dad on those same roads by the nursing home in Elkhart several times and was fascinated with his counting of the steps which he took and calculating the miles which he walked. It thrills me to recall that he was walking his last trip, even though it was at night and in a snowstorm, over those same roads.

Pneumonia resulted, and Dan was placed under an oxygen tent in the hospital on that very evening. Every time the nurses put the tent over him, he would sneak out of it. Because he refused to write on good paper, he wrote on a piece of toilet tissue a very meaningful sentence, "My life is not worth this cost." These were the words of a very brave man!

Dan's doctor needed guidance: Should heroic means be used to save Dan's life? Should he have a tracheotomy? The doctor-son, via telephone, suggested that they ask Dan. Dan's reaction was negative. The family believes that people who are dying should help make decisions such as this about their own life and/or death.

On Thursday, January 7, Lucy who needed to keep working for money's sake went as usual to see Dan after her day of teaching was over for he was always at the window watching for her. She realized that he was soon to die. He woke up sufficiently to smile at her and squeeze her hand, and then, within a few minutes he was gone, just as he might say a quick goodbye before leaving on a trip. The children feel it is wonderful to remember him as walking alone—something he always loved to do—shortly before he had to die. "Dad was his own man!" they say.

Viewing and visitation was held Friday evening, January 8, 1971 in Goshen. The body, given to medical research, was taken to the medical school in Indianapolis the next day. The Goshen community joined in a memorial service at the funeral home, meeting around a table brought from the family living room. On the table was an arrangement of wheat, oats, and barley and some greenery with a single candle rising from the center. Allusion was made to the perishing of the seed that new life may come into being. One of Dan's favorite compositions, "If With All Your Heart" from the oratorio, *Elijah* was sung. Several ministers participated in leading the assembly in the reading of scripture, in conversational prayers, and in witnessing.

A memorial service was held at the Manchester Church of the Brethren, North Manchester, Indiana on Sunday, January 10. "A Mighty Fortress Is Our God," sung by the congregation, affirmed Dan's belief in "a bulwark never failing."

To hear M. R. Zigler's tribute was to listen to a contemporary who had worked so closely with Dan that one could feel the kinship, the admiration, and the love which existed between them though their responsibilities in the church called for differing attitudes and actions. Let's listen to M. R. (age 80) as he just talks from his heart in a rambling kind of way: "And then along came this creative Dan West. He was creative. His imagination was tremendous. He was hard to live with, really. He was always so far ahead of me because I was an administrator and I saw the people in the churches and how much they'd do and wouldn't do. Dan couldn't see that. He only saw the distance: 'Where are we going?' And I had to somehow come along as an administrator to keep peace while he was tearing up the earth, so to speak.

"He had a unique way of going around, kind of creeping around here and there. You never knew where he was going to turn up or what he was going to say or what he was going to propose. But when it's all said and done, that's a good man to work with. It's hard on you, but you're always alive!

"The message of brotherhood which Dan West tried to give us, we didn't accept fully—the brotherhood within the church, brotherhood among the churches, brotherhood in the world. He suffered because a lot of us couldn't go along with him, and I couldn't go along a lot of times. I knew where he was going but I knew I couldn't get there quite yet. I wasn't ready to go; the Brethren weren't quite ready to go.

"Oh, how I'd like to go on with this idea of brotherhood. He saw the church as a great brotherhood, the church as it ought to be, not what it is, or was, but what it ought to be. That's what Dan West lived for as I understood him."

Passages of scripture, most read and appreciated by Dan—Deuteronomy 5:8-10; 6:1-5 and Matthew 5:17-22, 38-48—were read and thoughtfully interpreted by A. Blair Helman, President of Manchester College. S. Loren Bowman, General Secretary, represented the Church of the Brethren; and John F. Young, a Fort Wayne educator, paid tribute to Dan: "When God gave man a mind, he gave man the power to be creative, concerned, and responsible. Over the years, with the support of his wonderful wife and family, Dan West used this power by thinking new thoughts and by being concerned about his fellowman. And when he was called 'The Dreamer' it was the highest compliment from his many friends."

The family established the Dan West Education Fund to be used to support volunteers who manifest his spirit and who are able to give training in animal husbandry to recipients of Heifer Project livestock. The brochure for the fund states it well: " 'Passing on the gift' was one of the cardinal principles he [Dan] gave to Heifer Project. He believed that charity is degrading, but if you pass on what you receive, it is ennobling. Thousands of people have discovered the joy of sharing by 'passing on the gift' they received through Heifer Project.

"Many who had the privilege of knowing Dan West over the years also want to pass on gifts they received from him—

gifts of inspiration, vision, and hope." That they appreciated his contribution to their lives is attested to by the Dan West 52 Acres dedicated at the mortgage burning at the Ranch in July, 1977, and the fund for volunteers.

Letters of condolence and appreciation came from all over the world. From Rome: "I esteemed him as an ideal. I loved him as a man of great virtues. I pray for more like him. May all of you his descendants follow in his footsteps."

From Guatemala: "His work and efforts to develop Heifer Project have greatly aided the country of Guatemala, as they have helped most of the developing countries."

From a BVSer: "The radiance in both your and Lucy's faces which grew more beautiful over the years always spoke to us of the beauty of your marriage relationship, the Lights by which you live, and the blessing which your lives are and will continue to be to all of us who know you."

From Paul Robinson, then President of Bethany Theological Seminary: "I doubt if the Church of the Brethren will ever see another like him! And yet, in a very real way there are hundreds and thousands of us who are different because of him. Some of his unique style, his utter realism blended so perfectly with his never failing hope and optimism, and his passionate dedication to human values will live on in those of us who have known and loved him through the years."

A colleague put it this way: "What a man he was! One of God's originals!"

The late Andrew Cordier, then Dean of the School of International Affairs, Columbia University, said: "Few men have left behind them such a rich legacy of faith, conviction, and good works. The Christian principles for which he stood would, if applied, put an end to the major disturbances of today's world. His influence was deeply felt by many people in and outside the church. The extraordinary character of his life and the clearness and depth of his convictions mean his influence will be felt in the lives of people for decades and generations to come."

W. Harold Row wrote again of his appreciation and respect for Dan: "Dan has been a giant in the church and larger community—in a most un-giant-like way. Many of us recognize the important contributions he has made to us personally, but likely he has influenced us even more than we realize. Like all true saints, his charisma affects our lives subconsciously. Perhaps the Apostle Paul gives a deeper clue: 'I live, yet not I, but Christ lives in me.'"

"He was the only authentic 20th century prophet that I know anything about," said Joe Van Dyke, a long-time admirer. "He was a person with better than 20-20 vision; he saw himself and the society of which he was a part with such precision and clarity that reality and truth were his to a high degree. He was a person who lived what he believed, not just occasionally and impulsively, but continuously as a way of life. He was concerned not merely with his own life, but with all men."

Newspapers and magazines featured the life of a committed man, a staunch advocate of peace and an ardent student of conflict resolution. The *Goshen, Indiana News* put it tersely: "The Church lost a plain and simple man, who saw in every person a divine image; his goal in leadership was to enable others to let this image come alive." The editor of *The Evangelical Visitor* had heard Dan speak at a service club luncheon. Dan's idealism for settling differences between nations seemed impractical and unrealistic to him, but an editorial at the time of Dan's death asked, "Now as I reflect I wonder who was the practical one; who was the realist? Are not heifers more practical than guns? Is not love really more practical than hate? . . . Dan West was a dreamer of dreams and a doer of deeds. Not too busy doing to dream; not too busy dreaming to do. . . . There are of course others besides Dan West who demonstrate the potential of a man or a woman who is captured by an idea of a truth or a Person. The majority of us have an idea; or we have the truth; or we have found the Person. But from the days of the Apostle Paul to the times of Dan West it has not been those who had an idea or the truth or the Person to whom the world is indebted but rather those who were had by an idea; grasped by some truth; captured by Christ.

"Is it not the genius of the Christian faith that ordinary

people can do extraordinary feats when once they are willing to let go of God and let God take hold of them?"

In the Christian sense, Dan's death was a joyous occasion for his family. It was a relief for him to be free of the terrible crippling disease. Certainly there was a loss, a void, and that was deeply felt, but it did not make for sadness. The memorial services were interesting to the children, all but one in their 30s, as they listened to the extremely laudatory addresses. By this time there was a whole cultural environment in which their father belonged (including Heifer Project, church headquarters, and other groups in which he had been active) but to which the children really did not belong anymore. They felt a deep sense of pride in their father. Each had chosen a different path to follow, but they felt strong and warm inside knowing that their father had so successfully done what it was he wanted to do, that life had brought him so much feeling of worthiness. He was a very important and influential person to his children as well as to many, many other people. They had gained from him both some positive and negative things, but they were proud to be his children.

Of all of Dan's endeavors, it is the idea of the Heifer Project that the children admire most. In March, 1976, Heifer Project held a reunion in Plymouth, Massachusetts. Jan and her fourteen-year-old son drove down from Maine for the event. As Jan heard speakers from Guatemala, Honduras, and one from her own state tell about the heifers, sheep, and goats which had helped people become responsible and gain self-esteem, she was (in her own words) "amazed at how beautiful is this idea of giving the first offspring to another in need. What a simple and loving way. It has lived on and is becoming bigger; it's volunteerism, it's brotherhood, it's love, it's the key to getting along together in this world. My father came into focus for me in Plymouth. I could see beyond my daily frustrations. Then I saw what my father began with a new respect, and I very deeply appreciated being his daughter. It was wonderful for me to see that with my own two eyes and to hear so many speeches. I was fortunate to be able to see this down at Plymouth, Mass."

To Lucy, the years of Dan's suffering were heavy. Because

he did not accept his disease as fatal, the two of them could not, and did not, talk of death for him, nor of life for her after his death. It seemed almost a barrier between them. Yet she does not blame him, for he so often said, "I want to do more. I want to make history with ALS and I love life so much!" How then could one talk about death? "Here," she says, "idealism and realism never met." His death ended in an intense period of emotional stress. Lucy had to make plans, lists, and arrangements without even talking to Dan about them. This was hard, seeming almost untrue to him.

The community memorial service was worship for her; the service at North Manchester was full of praise, singing and rich in fellowship, a fitting closing for the family—a new beginning.

Lucy's thoughts about Dan: "I'm grateful to have been with him as wife, as companion, as one devoted also to the church but sitting on the back row. Even so, I felt I was helping him to do his thing. Someone asked after his going, 'Lucy, how can you love the church?' I must say that I never hated it because it called him away from home. Today I love it even more because I see and feel we need what he so much wanted—an intentional, purposeful following of the Master. Sure it's tough, but how else can it come? 'The grass creeps slowly up the hill/With faith that torrents cannot kill.' It seems to me now that we need so much of what he wanted. Maybe he was too early and too fast."

Such is the life of a prophet. Always challenging, sometimes warning. Loved by some who did not see all of him. Human frailties seen as pronounced by those who saw the 'tired part' of him. He wanted so much and tried so hard to be father, husband, companion after he had given "his all" to a task to which he was totally committed.

All prophets experience a sense of urgency, of impatience. Doubt and loneliness lurk in the background as their unique perspective is questioned and challenged. But the world needs prophets; the world needed Dan!

Among Dan's notes I found on a sheet of paper, yellowed, torn, and tattered, these words:

"Coping adequately with the present requires an understanding of the historic continuum. All previous history has made its markings on the graph, and we add ours to the continuum that the past forces upon us and from which we can deviate only when we have enough power to counteract its inertia. To determine what markings we are able to make requires (1) that we understand the directions and the momentum of the graph we inherit, and (2) that we assess the forces at our disposal to swerve it."

Dan wrote from Spain on December 16, 1937: "History has been alive since for me [referring to his college days], but now I care more and more to help make it." Dan's yearning was realized. He added his own impressive markings on the graph of history.